*Landscaping Earth Ponds*

# Landscaping Earth Ponds

## THE COMPLETE GUIDE

### TIM MATSON

Managing Editor: Marcy Brant
Copy Editor: Robin Catalano
Proofreader: Laura Jorstad
Indexer: Peggy Holloway
Designer: Peter Holm, Sterling Hill Productions
Design Assistant: Daria Hoak, Sterling Hill Productions

Printed in Canada
First printing, April 2006
10 9 8 7 6 5 4 3 2 1

Library of Congress Cataloging-in-Publication Data
Matson, Tim
Landscaping earth ponds / Tim Matson.
    p. cm.
Includes index.
ISBN 1-933392-02-9 (pbk.)
1. Water-supply, Rural—Amateurs' manuals. 2. Ponds—Design and
construction—Amateurs' manuals. 3. Landscape architecture—Amateurs'
manuals. I. Title.
TD927.M43654 2005
714—dc22
                        2005036025

Chelsea Green Publishing Company
Post Office Box 428
White River Junction, VT 05001
(800) 639-4099
www.chelseagreen.com

Chelsea Green sees publishing as a tool for cultural change and ecological stewardship. We strive
to align our book manufacturing practices with our editorial mission, and to reduce the impact of
our business enterprise on the environment. We print our books and catalogs on chlorine-free
recycled paper, using soy-based inks, whenever possible. Chelsea Green is a member of the Green
Press Initiative (www.greenpressinitiative.org), a nonprofit coalition of publishers, manufacturers,
and authors working to protect the world's endangered forests and conserve natural resources.
*Landscaping Earth Ponds* was printed on New Life Opaque, a 30 percent post-consumer-waste
recycled paper supplied by Cascades.

*To Jonathan, Hallie, and Katinka—*
*the original Loney Road pond gang*

# CONTENTS

*h*ow should I landscape my pond?"

It's a question I often hear, and there's no patent answer. Each pond is unique, a work in progress, ever evolving. Unlike the boilerplate demands of pond construction (water requirements, seepage control, inflow and outflow systems), landscaping invites a dance with nature. And everyone hears a different tune. One man's prize cattails are another's nuisance aquatic weeds. Nesting boxes for wood ducks, or pink flamingos?

Over the past few years I've found myself landscaping our thirty-year-old pond—in reverse. The monumental old yellow birch that commanded the north shore died and had to be taken down. Along the western embankment, a thick hedge of high-bush blueberries quit bearing fruit and shriveled up; off they went. These unkind cuts radically changed the pond landscape.

I spent a lot of time fretting about how to replace the losses. I gazed at the shorn scenery, lamenting nature's inconsiderate birth and death cycle. I walked the path around the pond, hoping for an answer to the question I'm so often asked. How *do* you landscape a pond? For sure, there'd be no replacing the century-old birch.

One day it dawned on me that with the blueberries gone, I could enjoy the restored valley view. Borrowed scenery, revisited. So instead of replacing the berries, I bought a couple of rustic cedar log chairs to take in the overlook. Then I added a second cherry tree at the south end of the embankment. A new view, a growing orchard, a vision of rebirth.

What about the yellow birch? I considered the bank of lupines under the missing tree. In the amplified sunlight they looked brighter, more vibrant. And so I held back the mower and allowed them to spread another twenty yards around the pond. The strong vertical accent turned horizontal. At the western edge of the lupines, I rebuilt an old beach with a truckload of washed white sand to establish a high contrast border (and improved swim access). A decaying landscape had been remodeled and renewed.

"How do I landscape my pond?" Look around: you've already started. Building a pond *is* landscaping. Put a new sheet of water on the ground and you're landscaping big time. You could stop there, if you wished. An elegant, unadorned pondscape is nature distilled.

But that takes considerable discipline. It's so much fun to play with nature. You might consider adding a spillway waterfall, not only for the rustic look, fluid kinetics, and planting opportunities, but also to switch on a liquid soundtrack. Or there's that embankment terrace—an empty canvas primed for pathways, wildflowers, grasses, native plants, shallow-rooted shrubs and trees, or stonework; perhaps even a sauna, gazebo, tent platform, or summer cottage. And if you're careful not to introduce invasive plants, there's a waterworld of aquatic species to border the pond edge.

*Landscaping Earth Ponds* is full of general strategies and specific examples of various approaches to pond aesthetics. You'll discover the pros and cons of various pond- and house-siting configurations to enhance your mise-en-scène; the unique landscaping characteristics of embankment and excavated basins; and plant, tree, and shrub selections for conditions ranging from moist edges to submerged shorelines. All accompanied by photographs and drawings to inspire you with examples of attractive design work. Translate them to your own territory, or let them kindle notions of your own.

TIM MATSON
Strafford, Vermont
March 2006

# ACKNOWLEDGMENTS

Special thanks to all the pond owners for permission to use these photos as landscaping inspiration; exploring and shooting the ponds was the best part of creating the book. Over the years, Marc and Ruby Lornell have been been especially generous with their design insights. Thanks also to the staff at the New England Wild Flower Society and Garden in the Woods; and to Phil Phillips of Timber Frame Joinery for his bridge construction saavy.

I want to thank my editor, John Barstow, for shaping up the text and helping clarify my thoughts, all with great humor and good energy. Margo Baldwin, publisher of Chelsea Green, deserves a special bow for taking on this project and exercising patience above and beyond the call. Marcy Brant, managing editor, kept the ship on course. And Peter Holm at Sterling Hill

Productions tackled the book layout with enthusiasm and an eagle eye. Finally, the entire project wouldn't have succeeded without unflagging support from Jonathan Matson, who kept the faith.

*Landscaping Earth Ponds*

# PART ONE

# Site and Landscape Design Fundamentals

# CHAPTER ONE

# *New Ponds*

*p*aradoxical as it may sound, there is such a thing as pond landscaping. You may have heard it called pondscaping, although that's a term usually reserved for water gardens and pools, especially those incorporating the rich variety of aquatic plants that can be used in small liner ponds. The large natural or earth ponds I'm concerned with make a bigger statement, and the land around them offers space for meadow flowers and grasses, perennial flowers, bird attraction, shrubs, and shade trees; paths, stonework, bridges, docks, and outbuildings; and even the sky.

"Less is more" is the favored approach to large-pond landscaping for many of my clients. The gentle arc of a dam, naturally curving shoreline, and liquid mirror reflecting the sky, clouds, and trees contribute to the tranquil natural effect many pond owners seek.

◄ Simultaneously modern and traditional, this pond makes it clear that building a pond is an act of landscaping in itself. The owners excluded aquatic plants and visual clutter like docks, rafts, and islands to enhance the sleek, liquid sculptural effect.

Earth ponds may benefit from aquatic plantings, but many pond owners are careful to limit invasive species, such as cattails, reeds, water lilies, and rushes, to edges and bays, making sure they don't overpopulate the main pond basin.

Some pond owners are reluctant to add any plants at all to the basin or shore of their ponds for fear of the damage invasive plants wreak, including choking all other plants out, root damage to the embankment, or attracting animal pests like beavers and muskrats. Some wetland designers advocate a hands-off strategy that allows native plants to populate the shores naturally, eliminating the expense and possible regret of importing plants unsuited to the conditions. Alas, this kind of laissez-faire approach rules out the sort of plant experimentation that can lead to attractive, manageable, and pleasantly surprising results.

Ponds intended for swimming, skating, and raising fish depend on good water quality, which can be quickly spoiled by invasive aquatic plants, or algal blooms triggered by plant nutrients, or fish food and fish waste. In pond landscaping, a careful balancing act is required.

Bottom line: building and maintaining an earth pond can be an act of landscaping in itself. After all, what's the difference between planting a tree and watching it grow and digging a pond and watching it grow? Much like a plant, a pond changes with age, weather, and the seasons. Leave it alone, and you may be perfectly content with Mother Nature's plan. On the other hand, like an orchard or a garden, a pond can benefit from smart, creative design, planting, and periodic maintenance to make it attractive and healthy. We'll look at both strategies throughout this book.

A bank of thriving lupines at my pond resulted from a chance mix of experimental gardening and just the right soil and southern exposure. ▶

## EXCAVATED VERSUS EMBANKMENT PONDS

First, let's look at the two basic pond types for a fundamental sense of their landscape characteristics. Whether you build a pond from scratch or buy property with an existing pond, you'll be dealing with either an *excavated* pond or an *embankment* pond.

Excavated ponds are built by digging out a basin on relatively flat, low-lying wet terrain and letting groundwater do the rest.

Embankment ponds are created by building an earth/clay fill or a concrete dam on the downhill side of a slope or stream to hold water back. Conveniently enough, the embankment is often constructed with the earth excavated during creation of the basin.

Excavated ponds are generally easier to build and landscape than embankment ponds (wetland permits notwithstanding). In

an excavated pond the groundwater flow is typically more predictable and reliable than the small surface streams of an embankment pond. Simple economical and efficient earthen spillways are commonly used, and they can be designed to include natural effects like stone bedding, waterfalls, and aquatic plants. There are few structural liabilities to planting trees on the shore of an excavated pond; not so an embankment pond. Trees and shrubs sited around an excavated pond create a narrative arc of seasonal colors and forms, from spring blossoms through autumn foliage. On the other hand, wetland sites and aquatic plantings make ponds vulnerable to water-weed infestations and beaver or muskrat damage.

◄ This excavated pond, as viewed from the house, was built in a wet hollow and relies on groundwater for its supply. The owner preserved trees to establish a foreground perspective and to create two distinct habitats, domestic and natural. Screening can also encourage wildlife.

▲ The dam used to create this embankment pond doubles as the driveway to the house. Aesthetically and environmentally, a gravel surface beats asphalt.

Planting trees and shrubs on a pond's embankment, however, is a bad idea, because roots can lead to leakage and erosion. In addition, pond embankment construction compacts the soil, creating tough conditions for many plants. Still, it is possible to plant shallow-rooted shrubs and plants on a pond embankment, especially along the outside edge in specially prepared soil. The broader the embankment top, the better the chance of planting far enough away from the water's edge to avoid problems with root damage and runoff nutrients.

When properly handled, the earthen terrace along the top of an embankment can be a dammed pond's chief landscape asset. It can serve as shoreline beach area, picnic ground, or simply a comfortable observation area for taking in the pond and its upstream landscape, or, with an about-face, a valley view below.

Once you're acquainted with the two earth pond types, you can intelligently evaluate pond sites (or existing ponds) for their landscaping potential.

◀ Extensive plantings around this excavated pond provide shade, animal habitat, and attractive surroundings, as well as privacy screening from a nearby road.

Although trees and plants are often prohibited on a dam because of structural and fertilizer runoff concerns, a vegetable garden lies safely below the top of this pond dam and benefits from a gravity-flow watering system. Livestock are fenced off from the pond to prevent water pollution and shoreline damage. ▶

## SITING THE NEW POND

The prerequisites for a good pond site include water-retaining soils (clay or hardpan), adequate water (groundwater and/or inflow from a stream or other source), and any permits from local and state zoning and wetland protection agencies. Plastic or clay liners and supplemental water can compensate for inadequate natural elements, but the job will be more complicated, costly, and often unsustainable.

A pond's size and shape are key to its site, aesthetics, and landscaping. Many people dream of a pond within view of their house. In northern latitudes the ideal house is oriented to the southwest for maximum heat and sunlight, so it follows that the best pond site will lie to the south of the house, if the terrain and soils there permit.

For more than two millennia, beginning in China and Japan, the sloping southward alignment of home, pond, and sun has been considered ideal both practically and aesthetically. When the sun is low in winter, you may even find yourself benefiting from its direct and water-reflected rays, barring snow and ice cover. The ancient geomantic art of feng shui carefully delineated house and pond landscape configurations to enhance health, financial success, and spiritual well-being. Sounds flaky, perhaps, but it's based on commonsense southern-solar orientation and good hydraulic practice.

Assuming you're fortunate enough to have a viable southward pond site, you can further enhance your landscape by orienting a noncircular pond with its long axis lined up with the sight line from your house. This optical trick makes the pond appear larger than a similar-length one oriented at a right angle to the viewer.

◄ In the best of all worlds, your pond site lies south and downslope of the house. Here the house, photovoltaic solar panels, and hot-water heating panels face south for maximum solar gain. These practical energy benefits of a southern orientation are complemented by the aesthetic bonus of overlooking the pond.

▲ The sight line from the house parallels the long axis of this narrow pond, an optical trick used to make ponds appear larger.

▲ A stone bench shaded by birches and echoing the shape of the pond also leads the eye down its long axis.

Whether a south-oriented pond is dammed or excavated, it is best located downhill from the house. This downhill orientation often lends itself to a commanding view, like a dune house overlooking the ocean. And there are practical advantages: A pond at floor level or higher can flood the basement or seep into it, creating chronic mold and mildew problems.

Let's continue with our ideal site. Perhaps the pond lies a couple of hundred feet downhill. The view is splendid. If the terrain levels off and it's an excavated pond, you'll have plenty of options for planting trees and shrubs around the shore to enhance the view and provide cover and food for wildlife.

If yours is an embankment pond, the dammed, downslope stretch of the shore is off-limits to trees, so don't be in a rush to cut existing trees along the upslope shore that might have landscaping potential. Adjacent fields also offer planting possibilities. And don't overlook embankment stonework, which can be a good stand-in for trees.

▲ Here a stone bench has been notched into a retaining wall overlooking a pond at Garden in the Woods in Framingham, Massachusetts. This is a clever way to transform functional into functional and friendly.

◄ Here are three views of an idyllic
small house overlooking its pond
to the south. The house sits above
the pond, which is nestled into a
natural swale on the hillside meadow,
allowing for a lower dam that does
not overwhelm the scene. The trees
are sited to provide afternoon shade
without blocking the view.

## SITING THE HOUSE

Now let's reverse our assets and imagine that you find a property with an existing pond but no house, or not enough of a house to be worth repairing. How do you site the house to best take advantage of the pond view?

Again, if possible orient the house north and uphill of the pond to create the classic southern alignment. Keep in mind, though, that you don't want septic system or roof runoff flowing toward the pond; likewise for lawn or garden runoff treated with chemicals or fertilizer. Lawn runoff is often a culprit in water contamination, with high nutrient loads leading to unwanted vegetation and algal growth. Site and engineer your driveway to prevent contaminated runoff from reaching the pond. It may be tempting to tap runoff from foundation drains and general household drainage, especially for ponds with water supply shortages, but such "trash water" compromises water quality.

I've seen too many properties with only a short steep lawn between house and pond, an arrangement with several drawbacks: It can be dangerous for children or the elderly, mowing may be difficult, and if the pond ever needs dredging or other construction the work site will be right under your nose. Erosion may be a problem, and if the pond is vulnerable to summer water level drops the ringside low-tide view may be less than ideal. Maintaining a little more distance in your pond relationship leads to longer-term happiness. I've even encountered a pond owner who found that close proximity to his pond led to seasonal insomnia, the result of high-decibel peeper peeping. My pond is a few hundred feet away from my house, and the spring and summer peeper and frog chorus is one of the annual highlights and a reminder of why I couldn't live without a pond.

I recall one home carefully sited and built to overlook an old farm pond. The house had large windows in the west end, overlooking the water, and a solarium facing south. The north side overlooked a valley pasture and wind-sheltering hill. The pond was dredged to remove decades of sediment, restoring depth and water quality. When the children were young a fence ringed the pond to keep them safely away. Household runoff and septic discharge were designed to flow away from the pond, and the basement foundation was set at a sufficient elevation to be safe from flooding. Homes built this close to a pond can be enchanting, but they must be thoughtfully designed so that they don't adversely affect the water, and vice versa.

▲ As the new owners saw it, this forty-year-old pond was the chief asset of the property. An old farmhouse downslope was torn down, and the new house sited and designed to create a waterfront home.

# CHAPTER TWO

# *Existing Ponds*

*W*hether you're considering a pond property with or without a house, thoroughly evaluate the pond before buying. Otherwise you may find that the pond is overdue for costly repairs, or you must face a hopelessly flawed structure. It's true that if worse comes to worst, you can build or repair a pond just about anywhere—permit exclusions excepted—but the cost may be substantial. The best fate for some terminally faulty ponds is to fill them.

Consider three basic elements when digging into a pond's pedigree: water, structure (including the basin, edges, inflows and outflows, and the dam), and history.

## WATER

Is the water clear or cloudy? Clear water is usually a good sign, unless you plan to raise warm-water fish, which prefer a summer algal bloom and aquatic vegetation to feed on. This can usually be arranged with the addition of nutrients, fertilizer, lime, and other ingredients. (See *Earth Ponds* and the *Earth Ponds Sourcebook*.)

Cloudy or turbid water may be problematic, depending on degree and persistence. My pond, for instance, is often a bit cloudy, which is to be expected because I stock crawfish to keep algae and aquatic vegetation under control, and they stir up sediment as they scuttle about scavenging for food. The water is excellent for swimming, and it clears in cool weather as the crawfish slumber and the photoplankton subsides.

Dense turbidity, often gray in color, may be caused by unprecipitated clay. Certain clays, once riled up (spring activity, inflows, fish traffic), remain in suspension indefinitely. Clarifying agents such as gypsum, hay, or other precipitants may help clear the water, but more elaborate measures might be needed—a liner or gravel. Remember that turbidity caused by recent rainfall, a passing algal bloom, or new construction is temporary.

Sometimes insufficient fresh-water exchange causes turbidity, and it can lead to stagnation, high summer temperatures, low oxygen levels, and algal blooms.

Dark brown–tinted but not cloudy water is often caused by tannic acid runoff from nearby pines and other conifers, minerals, peat, or submerged or buried trees. This taint can be tough to eliminate and is rarely worth the effort because the water quality is usually fine. Lighter brown water can indicate upstream soil erosion from roadside ditches or sandy streams. Turbidity of any kind should prompt questions for the pond seller about cause, frequency, and cure.

Algal infestation is a common problem and can plague a pond and make it unsightly and unswimmable. Algal blooms are caused by excessive nutrients in the water, stagnant or shallow water, sediment, and other factors. Remedies include cleanouts; eliminating pollution sources such as lawn fertilizer runoff; improving or increasing water inputs; aeration; and encouraging or stocking biological controls such as zooplankton, grass-eating carp, and crawfish.

Special dyes designed to prevent photosynthesis of problem algae and plants can be used. They require seasonally timed doses proportional to pond water volume. In ponds with significant overflow and without frequent reapplication, these dyes are short-lived, which is expensive and of dubious value to the downstream watershed. Dyes can also kill off the beneficial vegetation needed to support aquatic critters vital to healthy pond biodiversity. Some people like the look of a blue pond. I think it looks about as appealing as a reservoir full of Gatorade.

Pond water can also harbor invisible contaminants. If the pond will be used for swimming, check for bacterial contaminants, one of the most common of which is coliform bacteria. Contact your state health department to learn how to test for it. Other potential contaminants include *Giardia*, algal toxins, and cryptosporidium. Check to make sure the pond is not contaminated by runoff from septic systems, road drainage, or agricultural fer-

tilizer or manure. If the pond has heavy waterfowl or beaver traffic, the water may be tainted. If swimming isn't on your schedule, however, these matters need not concern you.

You may want to test for pH and dissolved oxygen, which are important to fish health, and for phosphorous and nitrogen, which can tell you if there's a potential nutrient problem that could affect algal and aquatic-weed growth. A reliable source of fresh inflowing water solves many water-quality problems. Aeration is another possible solution. Learning your water profile gives you a basis for comparison and helps you spot trouble early on.

◄ Several factors cause turbidity (cloudy water) in this pond: At the far end barnyard runoff is nourishing algae, and direct inflow from a feeder stream is adding sediment, as are areas of eroding shoreline.

## POND STRUCTURE

Whether your pond provides wildlife habitat or recreation, pay attention to the condition of the basin, shoreline, inflows and outflows, and, in the case of embankment ponds, the dam.

Begin with a quick visual check of the water level. Is the pond overflowing or is the water level below the spillway? It's not uncommon for water level to drop below spillway level for a time during warm, dry summer months, but if it's so low that the pond is unattractive, find out how often low levels occur and whether there's an acceptable explanation: new pond, drought, or recent draining of the pond. There may be an inherent flaw such as leakage, inadequate water supply, or both.

Do bear in mind that a pond's level and clarity vary depending on the season. In spring, levels should be high (if not, beware). Temporarily low water during summer isn't unusual, and autumn rains often restore levels. If the water drops during winter, the pond may have a leak or a supply problem.

Ponds, especially embankment ones, are often built with higher dam heights than the water supply can reach, leading to an unnatural and unattractive pitlike appearance. The problem can be remedied with an additional clay liner or plastic membrane to stanch leaks, or by piping in more water. Sometimes the easiest fix is to simply grade the dam to a lower level more consistent with the water level.

Ask the owner or take measurements to determine pond depth. The deepest area should be 6 to 8 feet or more, or the pond may not support fish, and shallow ponds, water temperatures, and oxygen levels may fluctuate enough to trigger algal and vegetation problems. Wildlife and wetland ponds, however, can succeed with as little as a foot or two of water.

◄ This badly eroding spillway was improperly sited in the middle of the pond dam; previously disturbed embankment soil is vulnerable to washouts.

### Edges

Examine underwater shoreline slopes. Shallow (flat) grades may encourage unwanted vegetation, while excessively steep slopes are prone to slumping. Shallow edges can be excavated to improve the slope; steep slopes are more difficult to improve without elaborate rebuilding. Keep in mind that steep slopes may be dangerous to young children. Shoreline work is best done "in the dry," with the water level drawn down for repairs.

If the pond has a sheet liner it should be covered with sand or other protective material. Also, sheet liners are often installed on top of a protective layer of sand or construction fabric and on top of underdrains. If liner edges are visible the appearance will suffer, and there may be leakage. Sheet-liner age and UV resistance will affect durability. Repairs or replacements may be needed.

Check the shoreline at and above the waterline for structural defects. Edges can be trampled by livestock and pets, or damaged by burrowing muskrats. Muskrat control may require live-trapping and moving the large rodents, or a protective liner of stone or fencing above and below the waterline. Low, wet shore-lines are especially vulnerable to damage, and may benefit from drainage piping (see illustration below).

Shorelines that are part of a wetland area are likely to be marshy by nature, and have the potential to support moist-soil plants. Cattails and reeds may be welcome in restricted shallow areas, but unless you're evaluating or planning a wetland or wildlife pond, they should not be trending toward a wholesale takeover.

Perforated plastic pipe can be installed to drain wet edge areas. To prevent clogging, drainage pipe is usually backfilled with crushed stone and protected by filter fabric. ▶

As many a pond owner learns, naturalized grasses can be a mixed blessing. Emergent grasses, especially taller species like rushes, reeds, and cattails, offer good habitat and food for wildlife, as well as water purification, and they help stabilize eroding inflows and discharge streams. But these same grasses can overrun a pond if not contained by manual weeding or dredging along edge areas, a daunting, ongoing chore. Containment measures include hand-pulling and cutting, water drawdowns, excavation, and bottom barriers. Herbicides formulated to kill aquatic plants are widely touted, but I avoid adding chemicals to the watershed. The invading plants will return, sometimes in greater numbers, and then you're hooked on chemicals. In general, allocate shoreline space to wetland grasses in larger ponds (1 acre or more). And beware of introducing invasive aquatic grasses you can't control.

Some pond owners leave shorelines unmowed. A band of wild-

◄ Windswept aquatic grasses add a picturesque element to this large pond, but they can quickly overrun smaller bodies of water. The older the pond, the more likely it will be host to uninvited grasses.

flowers and moist-soil grasses will usually naturalize along the pond margin, and the plants provide a seasonal succession of attractive blossoms and food and cover for amphibians, mammals, reptiles, and birds. In fact, many pond owners have found to their dismay that mowed grass invites geese, whose droppings quickly contaminate water and grass, and the longer they are allowed to stay, the harder they are to evict. An uncut grass or wildflower shoreland, with a narrow mowed path, may be the best design.

### Inflows and Outflows

Carefully examine flowages for erosion. If a pond is fed by an eroded stream or there's sediment accumulation at the inflow, repairs may be needed, including stabilization of the inflow channel, digging a small silt pool above the pond, and dredging out accumulated sediment. Learn the stream's source to gauge water quality. Where inflow pipes are used, they are often reinforced with stone and soil around the discharge outlet to stabilize

This detention pond holds water from a large watershed runoff stream before it overflows into the main pond below. In addition to de-silting the pond inflow, a detention pond reduces turbidity in the primary pond. Although often overlooked, detention ponds offer significant landscaping potential. ▶

against erosion and create a natural, camouflaged appearance. If your inflow splashes in without creating erosion or sediment, it can provide beneficial dissolved oxygen and the soothing sound of splashing water.

A pond's outflow system is one of its most important features. A well-engineered spillway prevents flooding and erosion; an ill-conceived one can lead to chronic problems or irreparable damage. Make sure to inspect the main pond spillway, which is often supplemented by an emergency overflow. Spillways come in many forms, including pipe systems, gated-control structures, and earthen channels. Establish that the spillway is functional and in good repair. In older ponds, steel or iron piping may be corroded and, if not already leaking, on the verge. If the pond includes a working drain, all the better.

A native, or natural, earthen spillway is a landscaping asset, much like a natural stream—but if constructed improperly, however attractive, it is an Achilles' heel. Simply adding riprap or gravel to an eroding spillway may only cover up the problem.

From a distance, this stone-camouflaged and -reinforced culvert pipe is all but invisible. The culvert was needed to access and stabilize a source stream that runs under a road before entering the pond. ▶

A new spillway built in an area of undisturbed soil may be the fix. Curving the spillway to traverse the discharge slope may help reduce erosion, but do not run overflow across a vulnerable embankment back slope, and resist layering a spillway with concrete; this leads to cracking from freeze-thaw cycles and to renewed erosion.

Be wary of unsupported vertical outlet pipes in deep water, where ice and water movement can weaken joints and cause leaks. Unsupported underwater drains can also be vulnerable to damage. Check the spillway pipe outlet to be sure there's no leakage around the outside of the pipe.

If the outlet end of a discharge pipe extends too far into the air it may be vulnerable to freezing and ice jamming. And be sure to ask if the pond has a record of beaver problems. Beavers can wreak havoc with spillways, and work may be needed to beaver-proof the overflow. Pest-protection "ratguards" may also be needed to keep animals from plugging a discharge pipe from the outside.

◄ Hefty flat fieldstones have been stepped here to stabilize a "native" pond spillway, preventing erosion and creating a waterfall with dramatic visual and sound effects. During the driest part of summer, the pond stops overflowing and the waterfall's structure is revealed.

### The Dam

Inspect an embankment pond by walking the dam and checking for signs of erosion or slumping on the surface, back slope, shoreline, and earthen spillway. If the pond features a pipe spillway through the embankment, look for erosion around the outlet and in the overflow stream at the foot of the dam. Erosion in any of these areas will have to be repaired, with corrective action taken to prevent further erosion.

Narrow dams or ones with excessively steep back slopes are vulnerable to erosion and possible collapse during heavy rains, snowmelt, and runoff. Check for signs of leaks at the base, or toe, of the dam, which may show up as saturated areas downslope of the dam, or more obvious leaks on the dam's back slope. Areas of unusually rich grass near the toe of the dam can be a leak alarm. A ditch dug parallel to and a yard or two below the toe of the dam can help reveal the location of leaks.

If the top of the dam is uneven or there are holes or caved-in slumps, the embankment may have been poorly engineered and

This dam has been breeched to draw down water and look for structural leakage. The dam was incorrectly built incorporating large stones, tree stumps, and other unstable pervious material. ▶

constructed, or may incorporate large stones or organic material such as tree stumps, which lead to leaks as they decay. Rebuilding a poorly constructed dam is an expensive undertaking. If you're considering buying a leaky pond, do your homework to determine the feasibility and cost of repairs.

Some dams incorporate gated spillways built of concrete or stone structures with wing walls and control boards to set the water level. Make sure there's no erosion around or behind the wing walls or under the base of the spillway channel.

Whatever the pond type, look for holes or other damage along the shoreline, which may be the work of burrowing animals such as muskrats or beavers. In time burrows can trigger leaks that lead to other problems. Even large crawfish can burrow deep enough around the edges to create leaks.

## HISTORY

Learning a pond's history can be as important to judging performance as any amount of inspection. Ask who built the pond and when. If the original contractor is available he or she will be a good source of information if repairs are needed. Ponds built with assistance from government agencies or private firms may have construction plans available for review. Survey maps and engineering drawings often detail size, shaping, embankment construction, spillway piping, emergency spillway, and waterline levels. Building plans can also be helpful in preparations for repairs and improvements.

Make a checklist of basic construction details. If the pond incorporates spillway piping, locate the inlet and outlet (seems obvious, but I often encounter people who don't know where the outlet is). If necessary flag the outlet so it doesn't get lost in the puckerbush. Other questions to ask include:

- Do the plans depict antiseep collars on spillway piping? If not, that may be the cause of leaking around the outside of the pipe.
- Is there a drain? If so, how does it operate? The ability to drain a pond facilitates repairs and weed control.
- What kinds of soils make up the pond bed? Soil composition affects water retention.
- Is the pond fed by underwater springs, streams, or both? It's important to know your water sources.
- Did the contractor encounter ledge during construction? Water following a ledge can cause leaks.
- Were clay or other soils or a sheet liner used to line the

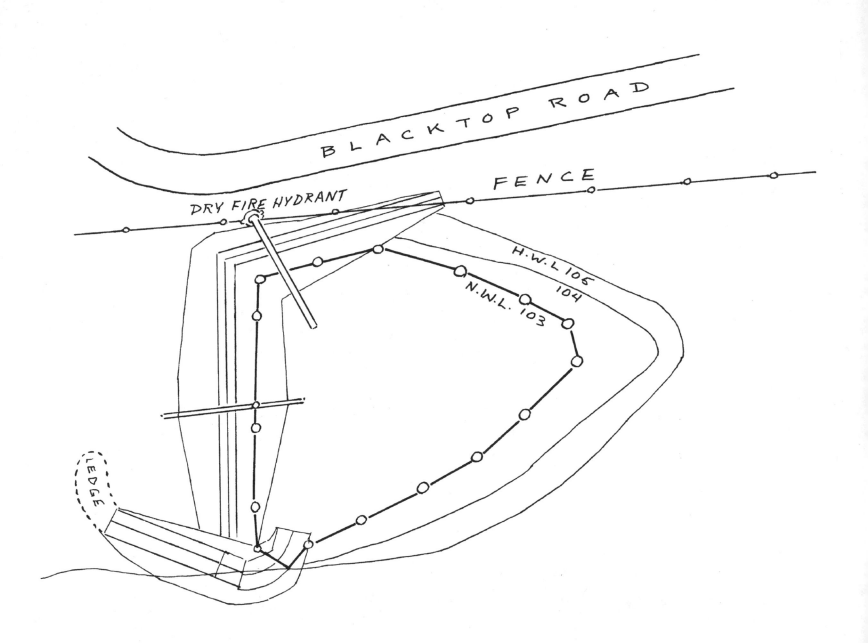

BLACKTOP ROAD

FENCE

DRY FIRE HYDRANT

H.W.L. 106
104
N.W.L. 103

LEDGE

pond? If there is a liner, were underdrains installed? Liners may need maintenance, especially after cleanouts.

- Were fish stocked? If so, what species, and how have they fared? Were they fed or did they live on native feed? Is there a history of fish kills, summer or winter? You may want to add or eliminate certain species.
- Does the pond have an aeration system? If so, how does it work? Aeration can improve water quality and the health of the pond and its inhabitants.
- Does the pond require supplementary water, and, if so, how does the system work? No water, no pond.
- Which critters now inhabit the pond (fish, beaver, muskrat, crawfish)? Get to know your tenants; you may need to serve eviction notices to some.
- Do above- or belowground electric lines or water lines run near the pond? Are buried utilities mapped? Search the records for all potential hazards.
- Do municipal zoning laws or state or federal natural resource conservation regulations govern the pond's use or repairs? Some states, for example, regulate aquatic-weed cutting, algicide use, sediment discharge into streams, fish species for stocking, and so on.
- Are there legal easements or deed restrictions affecting the use and maintenance of the pond? I once designed a pond on a site that turned out to straddle the right-of-way to an old, discontinued town road. One pond had to become two.

Many buyers of existing ponds assume that a pond takes care of itself—until something goes wrong. The more you know, the better prepared you'll be to make corrections and improve your liquid landscape.

◀ If you're considering property with an existing pond, find out if construction plans were drawn up and if they're available for examination. Plans like these Soil Conservation Service drawings can help you evaluate the pond and, if necessary, prepare for repairs and improvements.

# PART TWO

# Excavated Ponds

# CHAPTER THREE

# The Pond at Strawberry Hill

*t*he pond at Strawberry Hill is a fine example of an excavated pond designed and landscaped to combine a natural, rustic appearance with recreational, wildlife, and practical features. Strawberry Hill (the name has been changed to protect the owner's privacy) was built fifteen years ago by four families putting up homes on a large, jointly owned plot of land in Vermont. There was a good pond site in a marshy area some distance from the houses, which suited the owners, who liked the idea of a pond common to all.

When roads linking the houses were built, so was one leading to the pond site. A contractor was hired, and he brought in a dragline to dig what turned out to be a 1-acre excavated pond. Draglines work slowly, and construction took the better part of a summer and fall.

◄ Traditionally, wetlands made excellent pond sites, and a wetland similar to this was the original location for the Strawberry Hill pond. Nowadays, building a pond in wetlands usually requires permitting. Because wetlands are such valued ecological assets—filtering water and preventing flooding, among other benefits—state and federal laws and regulations protect them.

The finished pond includes landscaping features common to many excavated ponds—a shaped basin, wetland areas, natural stream inflow and native spillway, shoreland clearing, a spillway bridge, a path around the pond, and, a bit less common, an island. I thought it useful to begin my coverage of these landscape features as they apply to one actual pond. Considering real landscaping details in relation to one another helps present a coherent landscaping process. Later I'll discuss these features individually, and how they can be applied to various ponds.

◀ The Strawberry Hill pond combines a people-friendly shore and beach area, wetland preserves for native wildlife and aquatic plants, and a small island near the center. The island offers refuge and nesting areas for waterfowl, as well as a destination for swimmers and boaters.

Schematic plan of Strawberry Hill pond (not to scale). ▶

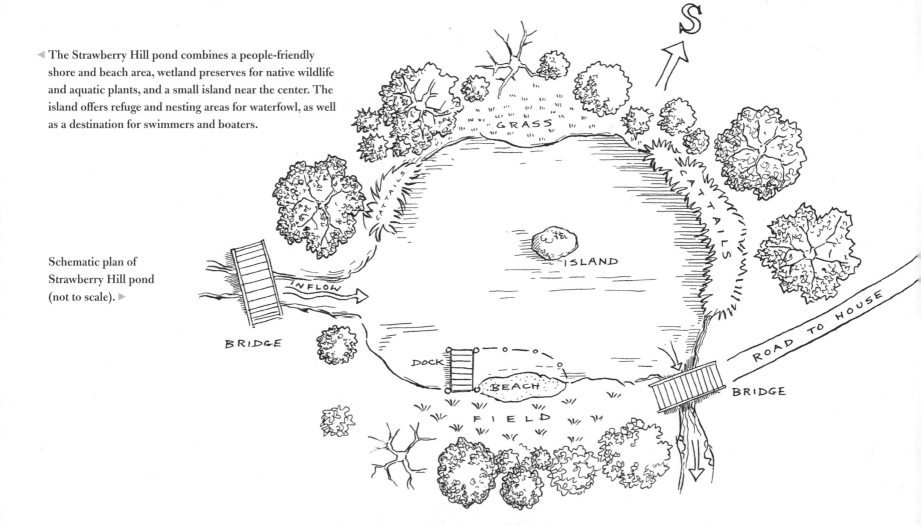

## SITING

The owners of Strawberry Hill were pioneers of a kind. Their tract of more than 100 acres had no electricity, and they set up solar and hydro units to power their houses. They built several miles of gravel roads. They also looked for a pond site in keeping with their back-to-the-land, off-the-grid style, and found it in a marshy highland bowl sheltered by high hills to the north and a view to the south. The area was generally flat, and they staked out a roughly circular shape.

The key is that they located a site for what I call a wilderness or destination pond, a quarter mile from the nearest house site. It was a place you could walk, bike, ski, or drive to. Or forget about, and leave to the wildlife. A place you could set up a campsite and wait for the moose, deer, coyotes, herons, hawks, and waterfowl to appear. Wilderness ponds attract more wildlife than those sited close to a house, and in this case wildlife was all but assured because the soils are saturated year-round—the area is a wetland. A few years later wetland protection laws would have required permitting for pond construction in such a site.

Currently permitting is often required to build in wetlands, depending on their state and/or federal classification. Clearly there are numerous strong environmental arguments for preserving wetlands, especially to prevent them from being drained and filled for residential, commercial, or road development. But a case can be made that transformation of all or a portion of a wetland into a deep-water pond is a plus for the environment. In much the same way that beavers created ecology-enhancing habitat with their ponds, human-made ponds can support fish and wildlife, control flooding, and provide fire and drought protection. And in a new era in which West Nile virus is a concern, transforming a wetland into a deep-water pond can be an effective way to reduce mosquito populations. Insect control was one of the original arguments for deepening wetlands: Deep edges and hungry fish are lethal to mosquito larvae. There's a big difference between turning a wetland into a Wal-Mart and turning it into a pond.

# CONSTRUCTION

At the Strawberry Hill site there was plenty of clay, revealed by test pits, and it seemed sure that the pond would hold water. The basin would be big enough—roughly 1 acre—for everybody to share. With the exception of a small pier, the residents agreed to build no structures onshore, in keeping with the natural surroundings. The owners planned to dig the basin about 12 feet deep so they could stock trout.

A word about those trout. At first glance, fish might not seem related to landscaping. But just as koi add visual sizzle to water gardens, trout have the potential to enhance a pond's natural look, especially a woods pond. The sight of trout leaping for flies and their sleek appearance near the surface and shore add to a pond's image, not to mention being an angler's delight. But several elements of the Strawberry Hill pond combined to make stocking fish a futile affair. Predators abound: kingfishers, herons, ospreys, otters, and perhaps even a few interlopers of the two-legged variety. And if those varmints don't finish off the fish, the native spillway, unfenced to avoid litter-clogging problems, provides a ticket downstream. Hence if you want to see trout in a remote woods pond, be prepared to restock frequently.

For every bucket of earth, a bucket of water: that's the basic formula for digging an excavated pond. As digging started, more decisions that would affect the landscaping aspects of the design arose. Everyone agreed that the shape would take its cues from the terrain. Wherever the land around the bowl began to rise, the digging stopped, creating a naturally curving shoreline.

Wetland vegetation in the body of the pond was removed, but one large cattail marsh was preserved at the inflow stream. At the time the cattails were preserved primarily to conserve native habitat to support existing wildlife. The cattail bay is also an attractive wetland plant area that adds to the overall natural appearance. It has proved to be a significant sediment filter too, reducing the silt load washing into the pond from the inflow stream. And shallow marshy areas at inflows are typical of natural ponds and lakes. Halfway around the pond a second cattail bay was preserved for habitat and landscaping enhancement.

Scientific studies have found that inflow waters running through wetland areas are purified by aquatic plants, whose roots and stalks absorb unwanted nutrients and pollutants, in addition to curtailing silt. As a result ponds are often designed—and existing ones modified—so that water enters through shallow wetlands, moves to deep water, and flows out at the opposite end. This flow line purifies and filters incoming water, and allows sediment to settle in the deepest area, reducing the

need for periodic cleanouts. Sometimes a "speed bump" is built up near the inflow, just inside the pond, to trap sediment.

What does water flow have to do with landscaping? Skillful water management improves water quality, which in turn reduces the chances for problems with algae and nuisance pond weeds. It's not much different from enhancing the soil quality for a new garden to minimize pests and weeding. Landscaping isn't only about how things look; it's about how they function. Preserving or establishing wetland grasses in the right areas can improve water quality and contribute an attractive landscaping feature to the pond. An ill-conceived pond that silts up and becomes choked with aquatic plants and algae that rob the water of oxygen leads to a fetid, unappealing, and neglected pond. You are better off leaving the existing wetland alone.

You must be careful to prevent designated wetland areas from colonizing large areas of the basin. While establishing and maintaining sufficient pond depth discourages plant invasiveness, manual control (cutting and/or dredging) may also be periodically required. Keep in mind that wetland vegetation may invite muskrats and beavers to take up residence, and they can harm the pond structure and water quality. You may have to take measures to prevent damage, including live or lethal trapping or building "beaver deceivers" to fence beavers out of the spillway.

We've been focusing on the pond—the hole dug into the ground. What about all of that excavated soil and muck? Scores of truckloads of material were dredged from the Strawberry Hill pond basin, and their disposition was key to a well-landscaped pond. With embankment ponds much of that fill is used to build the dam, but the Strawberry Hill pond didn't require a dam. Some of the fill was used to build up the low surrounding shoreland, which otherwise would have been soggy underfoot and prone to flooding. The rest was used for road building on the property and landscaping around the new houses. I talked to one of the original owners recently, and he noted with pride that none of the fill had to be trucked off-site. Using the material on-site eliminated the substantial cost of purchasing and trucking in landscaping fill and

◄ Excavated pond sites often support wetland vegetation, and many pond builders preserve areas of these plants voluntarily or as part of the permitting agreement. Aquatic grasses, like the cattails here, help prevent erosion with roots that hold the soil in place.

the cost of trucking the pond fill off-site. Especially for excavated ponds, plan for the best use of the fill, which may include building a road to and from the site; backfilling around a house foundation; and, on smaller properties, selling and trucking topsoil. It helps if you can use the material at home. When developing a new piece of land, a pond can be a landscaping asset in more ways than one.

The Strawberry Hill pond inflow wasn't significantly altered from the original stream that fed the marsh, but the outflow spillway required careful design and construction. As with many excavated ponds, a native spillway was designed, eliminating the expense and possible leakage problems common with an overflow pipe or concrete control structure. Using pipe would have required a large culvert and truckloads of fill to create a stream crossing, which would have added substantial costs and created a less natural appearance.

In addition to saving money, a native spillway adds to a pond's natural look; it's a re-creation of the way natural ponds overflow back into a watershed stream. Natural as it looks, however, a good deal of work was involved at Strawberry Hill. The spillway was sited at roughly the same place where the marsh originally

overflowed downhill into a year-round stream. To establish a water level somewhat higher than the original marsh, a large slab of ledge rock was positioned in the overflow channel to function as the crest of the spillway, resulting in an erosion-resistant discharge outlet. Fieldstone and other stone from the excavation was laid in the overflow stream below; combined with the ledge, an impressive waterfall was thus created. Enhancing the spillway

effect, wetland plants, moist-soil shrubs, and trees now grow alongside the waterfall and overflow, adding character as well as soil-stabilizing roots.

Over time, as often happens with new ponds, the spillway was reinforced against erosion by adding fill and stones to the sides to channel the overflow. A hemlock plank bridge strong enough to drive vehicles across was also constructed. A couple of piles of

◀ One of the highlights of the Strawberry Hill pond is the natural spillway at its west end. The owners preserved the overflow stream from the original wet area and added a hemlock plank bridge, creating an alluring, traditional "gateway" along the road approaching the pond.

▲ This small farm pond is sourced by a large watershed, with a wide discharge channel that looks out of scale with the pond. Installing an elegant custom-made pine and cedar bridge helped disguise the spillway and draw attention to the bridge, resolving the problem.

erratic fieldstone flank the approach to the bridge and pond, accenting the rustic effect.

Native spillways usually benefit from a bridge of some kind, if only a stiff board to keep your feet from getting wet. Bigger bridges may be necessary for lawn mowers, tractors, or trucks, depending on the size of the spillway, and they often require sturdy footings to establish a solid foundation in soggy soil. Bridges span the spectrum from simple wooden planks or logs to handmade arched wooden sculptures, like the delicate temple-style bridges you see at Oriental water gardens. Custom-designed and forged-iron bridge railings are also popular, as is cast iron. I've seen stone spans ranging from a rough slab of field-stone to a custom cut of elegant granite. Stepping-stones are used on occasion, although I'm not sure they qualify as a bridge. Various types of stone can be constructed in different styles by a mason. And I've seen an elegant hardwood bridge so prized by its owner that he trucks it away to the barn every winter to prevent weather damage. (See photograph, page 43.)

Of course, bridges aren't limited to discharge spillways. You may want one across the inflow as well, and it may benefit from visually matching the spillway bridge. Also wooden walkways, often laid out in shallow-inflow marsh areas, create access to the charms and complexities of a wetland. These are often built in zigzag fashion, snaking through the irregular wetland terrain and complementing the natural idiosyncrasies of the pond. I prefer to use naturally rot-resistant woods like hemlock or cedar over pressure-treated lumber, which has potentially toxic effects on the water and people in contact with the stuff. Recycled inert plastic decking is also gaining popularity, but it looks industrial to me. (See illustration, page 104.)

Eventually a shallow stone dam and pipe were installed in the Strawberry Hill spillway to capture water for a hydro system downhill. The electrical turbine charges batteries in one of the community homes. The pond-powered turbine is especially useful in winter when low solar energy is not enough to power the home. Ponds can also supply household and/or livestock water, fire protection (with potential for insurance premium reductions), irrigation, and geothermal heating and cooling.

◄ **At the other end of the bridge spectrum, this simple plank walkway gained a quick rustic character when the owner inserted soil and planted grass seed between the wooden planks.**

Dry hydrants are often installed to facilitate pumping access for fire trucks.

The shoreland around the pond is a roughly 60-foot cleared margin, which borders the mountain woods, a natural surround of hardwoods and conifers. The shore was planted with a conservation mix of grass seed, which took some time to become established in the compacted soil, but is now thriving. The grass is mowed periodically. The pond has had no beaver problems, probably because the large hardwoods surrounding the pond don't suit their appetites. And over the years a path was established around the entire pond, big enough for a tractor used to gather wood, mow, and otherwise pitch in on repairs.

In the entire pond design there is but one slightly off-key note: a small island in the middle of the basin. Maybe 6 feet across, like the tip of an iceberg, the island is too small. Proportionally it should have been about twice as big, and placed asymmetrically rather than dead center. Still, kids enjoy swimming out to the island to play.

Islands are tricky. They can have strong aesthetic and practical appeal, but they also present construction and maintenance challenges, and possible waterfowl problems. Of course, they add to construction costs.

There is an impressive list of island positives. In the right pond and when done correctly, they can look attractive, adding a natural touch, an oasis within an oasis. In a wetland or wilderness pond they lend an authentic look that convinces the visitor that this is a truly natural pond. Islands can provide refuge for wildlife and waterfowl, and they're often designed with nesting features for geese and ducks. They can be a platform for a campsite or campfire or even a cabin, sauna, or other small structure. Islands are usually isolated, or occasionally connected to shore by a bridge. Sometimes electrical service is connected to an island with a buried line.

◄ For folks living off the electrical grid, a pond can offer significant energy. This loosely constructed stone dam in the Strawberry Hill pond spillway impounds a pool of water that is piped by gravity to a hydroelectric generator downhill.

Considerations for island design include aesthetics, construction, and effect on water quality. It's common to make an island proportionally too big or too small for a pond. Too big and the pond becomes little more than a moat. Too small and it looks, well, odd, an off note in an otherwise graceful composition. If you're going to build an island, sketch out the rough size of the pond and pencil in the island. An island that takes up more than 10 or 20 percent of the surface is likely to take over the show. In my opinion, a pond smaller than an acre shouldn't have an island at all.

Islands can be built during original pond construction or later. In an excavated pond, an island might simply be an area left untouched during dredging. On the other hand, an embankment pond will probably require the island to be constructed. Either way, slopes should conform to the same parameters as the basin itself, and you should keep in mind that you are adding proportionally to the shallow edge area that can potentially support algae and vegetation. You are also adding to the area that can be a source of leakage, especially in embankment ponds, so proper compaction is important.

In general, islands should be graded at about the same elevation as the embankment or shore. You don't want it to look like a volcano. Depending on island size and pond type, you may be able to plant shrubs or trees, perhaps adding duck boxes. Remember that if it's a constructed island in an embankment pond, deep roots may trigger leaks, the same way they do in a dam.

Erratic stones or stonework can also be part of the island surface. In fact, I've seen islands constructed entirely of stone—big stone. As a bonus, the stone base is a haven for fish.

The waterfowl-magnet effect of an island can also work against you. One of my clients built a pond with an island intentionally designed as a waterfowl refuge. Unfortunately, instead of a picturesque pair of Canada geese arriving in spring or fall for a brief migratory layover, large flocks landed in spring and didn't leave. Water and shore quality was spoiled. And when the owners tried to chase them away, the geese flew to the island. Good for a wildlife or waterfowl refuge; bad for a recreational swimming pond.

Where waterfowl are welcome, islands are a common feature. If they're not built during original construction they can be created quite economically after a cleanout, using dredged material. In many wetland ponds these islands are little more than mounds of muddy silt, which seems to suit the birds just fine.

To finish off the Strawberry Hill pond, a small sandy beach and small steel pier were installed along the northern shoreline, where there are also a picnic table and a fire pit set back a few yards from the water. I would have recommended either a larger

beach or pier, or both. I gather that the modest sizes were the result of a compromise among multiple owners with differing design objectives. The beach was carefully sited in an area not subject to substantial watershed runoff, to prevent sand from eroding into the pond. The area is a gathering spot and overnight campground, oriented in the favorable south-facing pond alignment. However, no cabins or cabanas are permitted, in tune with the owners' rustic design, and as a discouragement to outsiders looking for a place to party.

To sum up the Strawberry Hill landscaping scenario: Dig out a saturated area (with wetland permits if necessary) and preserve some existing shoreline wetlands as wildlife habitat and to enhance water quality and natural appearance. Shape the pond to conform to the surrounding terrain, creating an irregular and natural-appearing shoreline. Preserve or create a shallow vegetated inflow area to help filter out nutrients and pollutants. If possible design the pond flow to allow sediments to settle out in the deepest basin area on the way to the spillway. Site the spillway downwind, if practical, to naturally help flush out leaves and other litter. Clear a band of shoreland around much of the pond to let in sunlight, and allow visitors to look out at the surrounding hills or sky. Build a native spillway without visible piping to add to the pond's natural appearance. Use native stone for the spillway, and accent cairns around the perimeter to help suggest a natural pond. Across the spillway add a hemlock plank bridge sturdy enough for trucks, in a traditional style that looks like it could have been built a century ago. Design the northern shore for swimming and general recreation, to take advantage of a southern-solar orientation. Build an island, if you must, but make it big enough to be useful and proportional to the size of the basin. And remember that most folks build a pond only once, so it pays to do your homework.

◀ In keeping with the remote-woods pond atmosphere, the recreation area is simple—a small beach and dock within swimming distance of the island. Note the eroded sand in the foreground: the beach needs an extra pickup load of washed sand every few years, but otherwise maintenance is minimal.

# CHAPTER FOUR

# Techniques

## SHAPING THE BASIN

*P*ond shape affects aesthetics and reservoir function. An attractive pond looks as if it could have been formed geologically. A round pond looks artificial; an asymmetrical pond with an irregular shoreline appears more natural. Natural pond shapes are as varied as the rise and fall of terrain. If you want your constructed pond to look at home in the landscape, avoid an artificial cookie-cutter look. Sometimes all it takes is a small bay or a point; giving the pond an irregular kidney shape is also effective. Simply preserving one or two elevated shoreland landforms may create an attractive shape. On the other hand, too many curves or too jagged a shoreline can create shallows and inlets that encourage excessively warm summer temperatures and consequent algal and weed growth. A variety of natural shapes, somewhere between the cookie-cutter pond and the chaotic perimeter, will

◄ Because excavated ponds are sited on flat terrain, they lend themselves to creative shapes. This pond evokes an Asian feeling with its hip-roofed boathouse, several bays of various sizes, and tree-covered island.

look attractive and enhance water quality. For example, Asian pond aesthetics stress the distillation of nature in shaping and landscaping in order to create a retreat and microcosm of the world. Or as one veteran pond builder told me, "I look at nature to learn how to shape ponds."

I usually recommend that prospective pond builders also look at constructed ponds for ideas, inspirations, and lessons. Take a tour of your territory, and be alert for ponds on your travels. Visit botanical gardens too. If a particular feature or design piques your interest, perhaps you can ask the owner or manager to explain its origin, construction, and operation. Remember to pick up the names of accomplished contractors as well.

Excavated ponds are easier to shape naturally than embank-ment ponds; with no dam they look more natural. Because they lie in more level terrain, you can make just about any shape you want. I've seen ovals, kidneys, and boomerangs, but most often it's a unique shape dictated by the terrain and surrounding land-forms. Preserving a tree or shallow wetland can lead to a distinc-tive curve or cove. Established trees around a pond site are a valuable cost-free asset, as long as their roots won't be damaged by construction or flooding. During your pond-assessment travels keep an eye out for features to avoid, and meet pond owners. I talked to a pond owner not long ago who needed to repair his eroded native spillway. One bidding contractor had shown him a pond with a 36-inch-diameter standpipe as an example of his fix. "It just didn't make me all warm and fuzzy," the owner recalled, adding that he wanted to impersonate nature, not industrialize it. He restored the original spillway.

Select one or more sites and experiment with perimeter design by staking out imaginary shorelines. Some people shoot photos of the site or make drawings, use surveys or computer models, and add overlays of various pond shapes to evaluate the different

◀ Preserving a single large pine tree along one side of this pond serves several functions. It adds landscaping character, creates a shaded destination espe-cially appreciated on hot summer days, and offers habitat for birds, which in turn help with mosquito control.

shapes. A topographic map with contour lines is very useful. Check out the pond from significant viewpoints (living room window, deck or porch, campsite, bedroom window) to evaluate sight lines and the aesthetics of shape.

As I mentioned earlier, varying pond shape or orientation can create optical effects. Viewed lengthwise, a pond with a long axis creates an illusion of greater size than if you view it at right angles.

Surroundings greatly affect a pond's appearance. A pond closely surrounded by trees can look smaller than one surrounded by rolling meadows, which permit more reflected sky to appear in the water. This effect is especially important to keep in mind when building or maintaining a small pond. Trees, especially big ones, can dwarf a modest sheet of water. This is a consequence not only of siting, but also of how you shape the pond in relation to its surroundings, and how and where you open up the perimeter area during construction.

◀ This small pond looks a bit cramped by its wooded shore, which has been allowed to grow unchecked over the years. There are plenty of good reasons to surround a pond with trees (privacy, soil stability, wildlife habitat), and excavated ponds are especially well suited to shoreline forestry, but the effect can become claustrophobic.

Pond planning includes considering which native trees to cut and which to keep. On the plus side, trees can have practical and aesthetic benefits, and it's important to remember that it's easier to keep mature native trees than to plant new ones.

When siting and designing an excavated pond, shorelines can be zigzagged to accommodate established trees, boulders, hummocks, and other features, and you don't need to be concerned about tree prohibitions on the embankment. Trees also preserve and create habitat and food for wildlife. Bats and birds can be a mosquito deterrent, a significant plus where West Nile virus is a worry.

A tree in the right place can also block out an undesirable view, so be sure that in cutting one down you don't expose something worse. It's amazing how even a single eyesore, like a telephone pole, can detract from an otherwise attractive landscape. The right tree in the right place makes excellent "eyewash."

Native white pines bowing over this excavated pond help stabilize saturated soils, especially alongside the discharge stream. In an otherwise open landscape, they contribute a wind buffer, a shaded grove, and a significant landscaping feature. ▶

In addition to shaping the shoreline, you'll be creating interior slopes. For recreational ponds, the best water quality results from slopes that range from 1/1 to 3/1. Remember, good water quality is good landscaping. However, the beach area will be shallower and close to 4/1 or even flatter. Carefully consider beach location; it has the potential to be an attractively land-scaped area where you may want a picnic table or level seating area, flower beds, or a place for your canoe.

Locate your beach on the north shore, to orient it toward the sun. Some prefer the beach to be one of the first places you reach on the path to the pond. For others privacy is more important, especially if they like skinny-dipping. Privacy can also be created with screening: plants or fencing or both. Ideally beach location combines many of these elements. Make sure not to site the beach where groundwater, springs, or runoff will create a mud pie or erosion. I also dislike beaches sited near parking areas.

Surrounded by an evergreen forest, this beach has an intentionally secluded feeling. A log cabin for camping, changing, and shelter gives the beach area a lakeside-cottage ambience. Although part of the pond is visible from the main house, this beach is tucked out of sight, adding to the wilderness feeling. ▶

There's more to building a beach than simply laying down a truckload of sand. For starters, it shouldn't be just any old sand; use washed masonry sand to avoid turbidity. A foundation liner (plastic sheeting or construction fabric) under the sand will suppress grass and aquatic weeds and prevent underlying soil and sand from mixing.

A beach can be more than simply a shallow slope covered with sand. Located next to a steep-banked peninsula, you can create a recreation area that combines a swimming area with a terrace for shoreline gatherings, picnics, barbecues, and diving. This requires early planning and stonework to build a submerged wall to support the peninsula. Put up a gazebo or pergola set back from the peninsula shore to make the area even more appealing. I've also seen peninsulas used for small cottages and saunas, and one decked off with a large wood pier. Peninsulas are especially well suited to excavated ponds because they may not need to be

◀ Spreading sand over a plastic or fabric liner prevents soil and sand from mixing. Beach sand also suppresses weeds. Use washed sand to eliminate silt from washing into the pond and clouding the water.

This beach combines a gradual slope affording safe access for children and the elderly, and a small constructed peninsula close by. The stone retaining wall was built to establish enough depth for diving. ▶

constructed. Have your excavator preserve a spit of land jutting out into the basin. Sometimes a peninsula can act as a platform for the excavator finishing up the dig, and is left in place. Peninsulas, as well as islands, can also be added later using materials excavated during a cleanout. Be sure to scale the size of the peninsula to the pond size. If it's too big it takes over; too small and it's an awkward bump.

Excavated pond construction may give you the most latitude regarding pond shape, but it presents a challenge in creating a good interior finish and stonework. If its water source is groundwater, the site may be saturated and pumping or siphoning will be necessary to allow the contractor to work in dry earth and create accurate, smooth interior slopes, or to set stone. Inflowing water may have to be diverted during construction, and if the natural soil is too porous a liner may be required. Keep in mind that liners work best in basins with a minimum of tricky angles. Sheet liners usually need both a protective foundation and cover to prevent punctures, decay, and groundwater displacement under drains. Some larger excavated ponds in flooded sites are dug by dragline, but finished basin slopes will not be as smooth as one dug in the dry. In my experience contractors usually create curving shorelines as they dig, although

some find it easier to excavate squares or rectangles and round off the corners at the finish.

Unlike embankment ponds, which use excavated material in the dam, fill from dugouts must be removed from the site or, better, used for shore construction and general landscaping. Make plans for the disposition of excavated soil prior to starting the job. If you don't ship it off-site (which has the potential to generate income) consider these uses around the pond.

Fill may be suitable to build up the shore area, which can be soggy around excavated ponds. Porous, not too silty soil can be spread around the shore to create a well-drained perimeter suitable for planting grasses, shrubs, and trees. Excavated soil is usually set aside to drain before use, and silty loam may not even drain well enough to be used for shore material. In extremely wet areas, underground drains may be necessary to dry out the shore-land. (See illustration, page 23.)

◀ Building a peninsula for your pond can add significantly to the design, whether it's a subtle naturalistic curve or a more dynamic jut of land like this. Here stones removed during construction are used as optional cladding to protect the peninsula against erosion; a different designer might prefer an earthen foundation.

▲ This sweep of lawn was built up using material excavated from the pond. Although sometimes called waste, earth dredged from a pond site is a valuable asset.

◄ Low water exchange in this pond has encouraged invasive plants and algae. Proper pond depth and basin slopes are also important in averting unwanted vegetation.

Use fill to create hills or "privacy berms," to shield the pond from neighbors, roads, or other public viewpoints, as well as from traffic noise and other sounds. Create surroundings that appear natural and with gradual enough slopes to prevent erosion. These hills also serve as shelters from prevailing wind and snowdrifts. Don't build artificial hills or store fill too close to the pond's shore, where the weight of the soil can crush the pond edges or erode into the water. The same goes for keeping excavated material back from the edge of test pits that won't be immediately refilled. Neither should surplus fill be deposited in pro-

tected wetlands, which can be a serious violation of state and federal wetland protection laws. If it looks like excavated material will have to be trucked off-site, be sure construction plans include provisions for a proper haul road and disposal.

Because excavated ponds often rely on groundwater and lack a decent inflow source to create an exchange of new water, stagnant conditions can result. Consequently, summer's high water temperatures and low dissolved oxygen levels invite algal growth and aquatic weeds. Throughout much of the country, ponds should be at least 8 feet deep, with 10 feet or deeper preferable. Deeper water means cooler water means cleaner water. Water quality can be improved by encouraging biological activity, including certain types of fish, crawfish, and zooplankton. During planning and building of an excavated pond, take measures to ensure an exchange of fresh water. A supplementary source of water may be required, perhaps pumped in from a nearby stream or dedicated well. Upstream sources are often tapped by gravity for extra water, including springs and groundwater piped in by underground field-drainage pipes.

A cabin secluded in the trees exemplifies the camouflage style many waterside cottage owners choose in order to preserve the wild nature of their ponds. Hardwoods switch on a grand tableau of color every fall. ▶

Aeration systems also improve water quality. In many people's eyes they provide visual enhancement as well. Although not as effective at adding oxygen as invisible underwater diffusion systems, fountains do improve dissolved oxygen levels and add a dramatic visual effect. Water- or air-pumping windmills improve water quality and introduce a distinctive look. Aerators improve water quality by destratification, which mixes water temperature layers to prevent low-oxygen dead zones that lead to fish kills and algal blooms.

Trees shedding their leaves into the pond contribute more organic nutrients and may need to be trimmed back. As I've said, good water is good landscaping.

Of course, if you're designing your pond as a wetland feature or wildlife habitat, you'll probably want a much shallower basin (2 to 3 feet), and some pond owners incorporate shallow areas as part of larger recreational ponds. Wetland vegetation in these areas can enhance a pond's appearance, support wildlife, and improve water quality; or it can backfire and encourage the spread of unwanted invasive aquatic plants.

Careful planning should precede the creation or planting of shallow areas.

As you stake out your pond, consider the preservation of natural surroundings as a landscaping asset. Trees may need to be cut to clear the site and shore perimeter, but don't go overboard. Unlike a sunny pasture pond, a woods pond can create an out-of-reach wilderness mood. Trees are natural privacy barriers and buffers against noise, and they surround the pond with wildlife habitat. Nearby trees enhance the natural appearance of the pond and serve as view "frames," and are sources of shade and privacy.

When in doubt, postpone tree felling until you've lived with the pond for a spell and are certain about which trees you want to remove. Even a dead or dying standing tree can be an asset, providing habitat and food for birds and other critters. That goes for dead and downed ones as well. A landscape contractor I know occasionally has to locate a dead tree to fetch for a client's pond to add a naturalistic effect. A dead tree lying in the shallows at the edge of a pond is also valued by turtles and frogs seeking a sunbathing perch. Recently I visited a new pond shaped to include a peninsula covered with old maple trees. Had the trees been cut and the peninsula excavated, the pond would have been far less attractive, not to mention absent of any shady areas.

As you design the perimeter, imagine yourself walking around the shore. A path around the pond offers a variety of interesting views, as well as site-specific landscaping possibilities. A small change in siting or perimeter shape may allow you to take advantage of a potentially interesting pond path.

Paths can range from elaborate stone-paved walkways to elegantly curved alleys mowed through tall grass. A single pond may combine a variety of these landscaping features. Many pond owners avoid crew-cut mowing to encourage shoreline grasses, wildflowers, and wildlife habitat. Grasses, shrubs, and trees add to the pond's character and offer potential privacy screening. Limited cutting is also a great excuse for not firing up the lawn mower.

Consider enhancing a curved shoreline with a sandy beach cove, a wetland vegetation bay (cattails, rushes, and so forth), or a simple inlet. I visited a pond not long ago where a small stone-edged inlet was used as a docking area for a rowboat.

◄ One of the most rewarding elements of landscaping is a path encircling the pond. Such a trail can take you to attractive viewing points and interesting features, such as flower gardens, inflow and outflow streams, waterfalls, a dock or bridge, a boardwalk over wetland areas, plants and trees, stonework, benches, and more.

When complete, this mooring inlet will be a sheltered tie-up for a small boat. The stone prevents erosion and will tone down in appearance over time. ▶

If a shoreline feature is not incorporated in the original construction, the best follow-up work is usually done while the water is drawn down in the work area. Excavated ponds offer lots of options for shoreline remodeling because there's no dam to preserve. Drawdowns are accomplished by siphoning with a pipe or hose, or by pumping. Diverting inflows, if possible, or working during a low-water dry period also helps.

Unless intentionally designed, shallow areas should be minimized, monitored, and maintained to minimize algae and aquatic weeds, and prevent growth from spreading into the main basin. Fortunately, shallow beaches are self-maintaining. The sand, and foundation liner if used, mulches out plant growth in what would otherwise be ideal territory for aquatic vegetation.

If stonework is in your future, discuss preparations with your contractor. Stone can be used in the construction of a peninsula, steps into the water, a diving stone, pipe reinforcement, edging, stabilization of inflows and outflows, a bridge, an island, fish habitat, waterfalls, retaining walls, edging, paths, benches, diving platforms, and more.

The combination of stone and water unites nature's extremes, creating an image and sensation of unity for the visitor. And as a building element, stone outlasts other materials—a legacy for the ages. Choice of stone—fieldstone or a quarried, commercial type—depends on indigenous stone and your design intentions. It's easy to inadvertently create an unnatural appearance by using the wrong sort of stone.

Stonework in the pond itself often requires working "in the dry," and preparations have to be made to cut off inflows or to pump or otherwise draw down water levels. For stonework to be stable the foundation work is usually done on a prepared slope or shelf designed to eventually be underwater, and larger stones are used as a foundation.

To create shoreline edging that's flush with the grass the stones should be carefully leveled using a transit. For diving stones and other larger installations keep in mind that bigger stone tends to stay put.

Excavated ponds are more likely than dammed ones to have native spillways, which can benefit from stonework to reinforce the channel against erosion. Using local fieldstone or stone of a color that blends with native stone is preferable to importing off-color or off-texture stone. Stonework is an art, so make sure your stonemason is up to snuff.

Piped runoff from a large watershed feeds this handsome pond, which is stabilized against erosion by its stone retaining wall. Water quality is improved because the vertical wall increases the pond's depth and volume. The wall also allows for a garden terrace. ▶

## PLANTING

Excavated ponds allow you more latitude regarding planting than embankment ponds. Trees and shrubs can be introduced without concern about root damage to a dam. A pond excavated in an open field will benefit from one or more trees thoughtfully placed for shade, and from plants used for fruit, wildlife attraction, and general landscaping. Trees and shrubs create privacy and sound buffers; tall ornamental grasses can be used for screening as well as an alluring appearance. Ponds in suburban areas may present safety and liability concerns, so a fence may be required. Otherwise a hedge of wild rugosa roses makes an attractive and nearly impenetrable barrier.

Keep in mind that tree roots do have the potential to compromise piping. Willow trees, for example, are notorious for damaging everything from foundations to septic systems, and willow leaf litter can be an unwelcome source of debris and nutrients in the water. (See part 4.)

A line of flowering crab apple trees and a split-rail fence establish a visual property line and subtle privacy screen. It's an elegant compromise between a barricade and an open field. ▶

# PART THREE

# Embankment Ponds

# CHAPTER FIVE

# *The Lornell Pond*

*e*mbankment ponds involve more complexities in design and execution than excavated ponds, so it's a challenge to choose just one of my many favorites as a representative model. Nonetheless, the quarter-acre Lornell pond does embody many of the best characteristics—and challenges—common to embankment pond landscaping.

## SITING

Sited less than 100 feet downhill from the house, the pond is the dominant landscape feature. The passive solar house faces south toward the kidney-shaped pond, with views from the first and second floors, the flagstone terrace, and the gardens. The pond

◄ Building close to the water, the Lornells live a pond-focused life. With its expansive solar windows and two-story living room and balcony, the house is a pond theater.

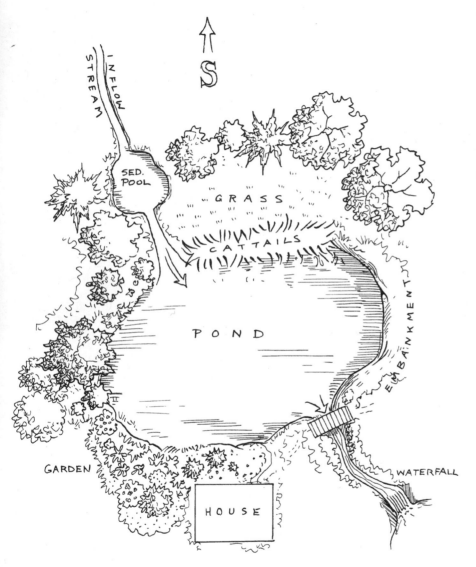

▲ Schematic plan of the Lornell pond (not to scale).

scene changes with every rainfall, wind shift, turn of light and season, and movement of animals and birds. There's a shifting soundtrack too, season after season, day and night: rainfall on the water, twilight peepers, jumping fish, cracking ice, water splashing down the spillway.

The pond and house were built simultaneously, and it's unlikely that anything but an embankment pond located downhill from the house could have been built so close to it. In fact, an excavated pond so near a house on level terrain would likely flood the cellar.

The pond lies in a draw that slopes away to the right (west), where the dam was constructed. The view beyond the quarter-acre pond is a sidehill of carefully managed mature hardwoods and conifers. The water source for the pond is groundwater and springs on the site. An upslope detention basin invisible from the house captures watershed runoff, settles sediment, and holds a backup water supply that feeds surplus water down a stone-lined waterfall into the main pond. In addition to being an attractive stonework cascade, water tumbling down the channel is aerated, adding a healthy dose of dissolved oxygen to the pond.

The view from the Lornells' deck. On sloping terrain an embankment dam is necessary to complete the pond basin structure. Here the dam (right) becomes an asset as a lawn and part of the pathway around the water. ▶

Although ponded water might seem to be the prime focus, embankments themselves have equal potential to become attractive and usable attributes. That's what makes embankment ponds so different from excavated basins. Embankments have the capacity to become elevated gardens, scenic overlooks, beach areas, and sites for a variety of structures, from tents to cottages and more.

The potential for mirroring, pro and con, should also be considered during pond design. For example, a grove of white birch trees across the Lornell pond reflects vividly in the water; a telephone pole in the same area would also show up not once but twice.

Opposite the Lornell dam, the eastern upslope is steep, scattered with native rock, and covered with flowers and shrubs, many in terraces built up with fieldstone retaining walls. A path of stepping-stones leads from the house around the eastern shore of the pond, past this rainbow of flowering plants and shrubs. At the far end of the pond, the visitor steps onto the grassy dam to begin the walk back to the house, crossing the spillway bridge just before returning home.

## THE DAM AND BASIN STRUCTURE

The waterline along the dam is only a foot below the top of the embankment, creating a pleasing proximity to the water. Such high-water effects can require oversize discharge systems to make sure overflow during peak runoff periods doesn't breech the dam. A secondary emergency spillway installed at another location along the dam or shore ensures that floodwaters do not overtop the dam itself. The Lornell pond's spillway is large enough to handle peak runoff, but a low grassy spillway area was also created to handle flood runoff, just in case.

An aluminum sculpture with a long hinged pinion seesaws in

The Lornell embankment skimps on freeboard in exchange for a "brimful effect," considered an aesthetic advantage by some pond owners. Low freeboard enhances the mirror effect by minimizing the height of the embankment above water level, and reduces the stripe of embankment reflected in the water. ▶

slow motion in the breeze, like a heron's beating wing, at one end of the embankment. Thus, as it does at many ponds, the embankment doubles as a sculpture garden.

The path around the pond winds up at an iron-and-wood footbridge that spans the spillway. Crossing the bridge, the visitor's natural instinct is to stop and watch the overflow cascade down the stone spillway waterfall. Although not an arched bridge, it is high enough above the spillway to give the viewer a dramatic, elevated viewpoint of the tumbling water. Lofty viewpoints were also valued by Oriental-garden designers, who built arched bridges not only for the aesthetically pleasing image they presented, but also for the elevated view of the pond and surroundings.

Native spillways for embankment ponds are often sited at either end of the dam for structural solidity. The Lornells chose the end nearest the house to have the waterfall view and sound as close as possible. The spillway also lies across the pond from the main inflow, which sets up a current favorable to water quality. Avoid siting an inflow near the spillway. It can lead to silted-up overflows and poor water circulation. This applies to piped overflows as well as native spillways.

The Lornells are avid gardeners and have done much of the landscaping themselves. Ruby Lornell created the flower gardens, and her husband, Marc, did the stonework and woods maintenance, with help from a bright orange Kubota tractor.

This is an interesting example of embankment pond landscaping, for several reasons. The Lornells were able to transform an unruly, steep front-yard ravine into an attractive waterfront, as well as an ongoing landscaping project, which fills many creative retirement hours.

The handsome high waterline—the "brimful effect," as they

◀ Native embankment spillways are usually sited at either end of the dam. The Lornells chose the location closest to the house to be near the sound of a waterfall and other landscaping assets, including stonework, moist-soil plants, and a custom-made footbridge—all of which would have been impossible with a piped discharge.

▲ Above the main pond, a detention pool collects watershed runoff and stream water, doubling as a water source and a sediment filter.

call it—wouldn't have been feasible without a capacious spillway/waterfall to handle peak capacity runoff, which in turn has aesthetic benefits of its own. Some pond contractors might have opted for a drop-inlet pipe, but that would have required a large and, to many eyes, unattractive pipe. True, it could have been camouflaged under a pier or stone shelf, but the attractive waterfall spillway would have been lost.

And finally, an area that often winds up as a rough off-limits watershed above embankment ponds has been transformed into an attractive stone-terraced rock garden.

## ANATOMY OF A DAM

Dam construction begins with the removal of topsoil throughout the foundation area and the creation of a core trench. The core trench should be deep enough to get below sand to clay or bedrock; the sides can be slanted or vertical. If your best clay material is in short supply, be sure to use it on the front half of the dam.

Material around pipe spillways should be thoroughly compacted to eliminate air pockets. Antiseep collars are also essential to prevent leaks. The drop inlet should be located close to the shore to take advantage of the earth reinforcement, which is especially helpful against ice damage. If you include a drain, reduce the size of the spillway pipe to prevent downstream erosion during drawdowns. Be sure the drain intake is high enough above the pond bed to prevent burial in silt. Most ponds incorporating piped spillways also feature a secondary or emergency spillway to carry away floodwater that exceeds pipe capacity during unusually heavy runoff periods. The emergency spillway is usually an earth-cut channel 1 to 1 1/2 feet above the principal spillway inlet, with the top of the dam another foot or so higher still.

The interior and exterior pond slope angles surrounding a dam will affect structural integrity and longevity, aquatic vegetation, and embankment maintenance. As shown below, 3 to 1 is a generally durable basin slope. Slopes should range between 2 to 1 and 4 to 1.

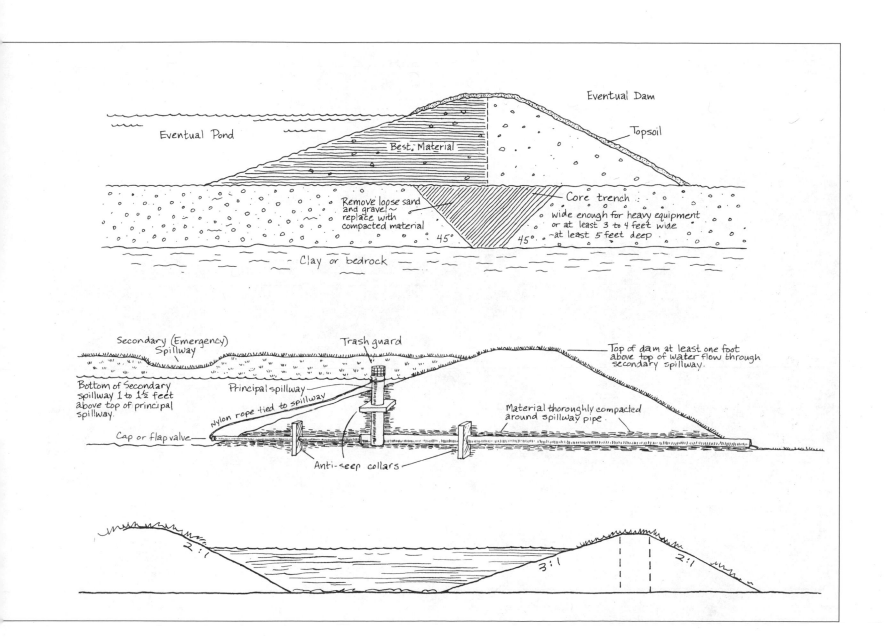

Eventual Dam

Eventual Pond

Topsoil

Best Material

Remove loose sand and gravel ~ replace with compacted material

Core trench
wide enough for heavy equipment or at least 3 to 4 feet wide ~ at least 5 feet deep

45°    45°

Clay or bedrock

Secondary (Emergency) Spillway

Trash guard

Top of dam at least one foot above top of water flow through secondary spillway.

Bottom of Secondary Spillway 1 to 1½ feet above top of principal spillway.

Principal spillway

Nylon rope tied to spillway

Material thoroughly compacted around spillway pipe.

Cap or flap valve

Anti-seep collars

2:1

3:1    2:1

# CHAPTER SIX

# *General Techniques*

## SITING

*i*f your pond site is on sloping terrain you're going to need a dam. The steeper the slope, the higher the dam. And often the bigger the pond, the bigger the dam. Because the dam is likely to be a bulky artificial structure, it's important to imagine its appearance from various angles. Avoid the military bunker look. On the other hand, don't skimp on the dam top.

Ideally your principal view will be from above the pond or roughly level with the dam. A house sited below a dammed pond is unlikely to yield a great prospect, and depending on proximity might be vulnerable to runoff or flood damage. The view of a dam in a location you can't see from the house is less critical.

If you hope to construct a dammed pond in view of an already existing house, be sure you've got a good pond site with adequate water sources (groundwater, stream, or both) and good soil.

◄ This 1-acre embankment pond lies about 100 yards below the owner's home. Originally a damp area that was difficult to mow, the pond is both a solution to a drainage problem and a landscaping improvement.

Lacking natural ingredients, you'll need to create a supplementary water supply (well, pumped stream water, springs, field drainage) and/or use a liner (clay, sheet liner, or other sealants). These efforts to improve on Mother Nature are not foolproof or free. Whatever the site's characteristics, hire an experienced contractor, preferably one whose ponds you've seen and liked. It's helpful to discuss neighboring pond construction strategies and costs for comparison with your own plan. The last thing you want to do is create a 10-foot-deep pit of frustration just beyond your dooryard.

Recent changes in federal and state wetland protection laws encourage pond builders to site ponds in upland meadows to avoid damage to wetlands. These locations generally require embankment construction, not to mention an often challenging search for an adequate water supply. This increased emphasis on embankment ponds in poor-water areas is all the more reason to work with an experienced, trustworthy contractor who has the integrity to say no if the project looks too risky. Well construction is also on the rise, in connection with upland pond projects, so you may need to talk to a well driller. If your household well has especially good flow, there may be a chance to link it to the pond.

I worked on one pond where the owners benefited from waiting for more than a decade to build the pond, and were consequently well acquainted with the reliable character of the groundwater and runoff in the site, as well as low-infiltration soil, which gave them the confidence to proceed with the large project. (See photograph, page 80.) A pine tree was preserved as a landscaping accent and to hold together soil in the feeder-stream area, where runoff funnels into the pond. Preserving a tree at the inflow area is a conservation measure I often see, and it yields both a landscaping feature and erosion control. It's comparable to preserving wetland vegetation in the inflow area. In some ponds you can do both. At this pond the natural look is emphasized by the absence of any shoreline construction—pier, swim raft, or building. The graceful curve of the dam echoes the

Here is another embankment pond in a traditional house-and-pond configuration, but with an entirely different character. The ambience is mountain get-away, with the main house overlooking a pond that features a summer-camp–style cottage with dock, boats, and a swim raft. (Cover the cottage with your hand or a piece of paper to see how much a shoreline structure affects the landscape style.) ▶

shape of the distant hills and rolling pasture terrain; the quarter-moon shape conforms to the contours of the hill.

For entirely different ambience, ponds can be embellished with buildings, recreational paraphernalia, and flower gardens. Shoreland buildings run the gamut from waterfront homes to boathouses, cottages, cabins, lean-tos, saunas, and more. Whether you use the embankment itself as the structural platform will depend on a design that minimizes the impact on dam integrity.

If you are building a house near an existing pond, so much the better. It's usually easier to find a good home builder than a good pond site and experienced contractor. Hence the high value of existing ponds. Buyers of older ponds often believe that maintenance of some kind is required to put their stamp of ownership on it, but this is not always true.

I visited one embankment pond where the house overlooked the water—and three decades' worth of cattails, reeds, and other aquatic vegetation. The new owners were pond novices, and I've seen many neophytes take it for granted that a basin so old and weedy needs a dredging. But after some consideration, they chose instead to preserve the naturalized aquatic vegetation. The pond

had evolved into a shallow wetland and wildlife habitat, and they valued the richness of plants, birds, fish, and frogs. The pond symbolized what they loved about country living. It wasn't a recreation pond they were seeking, but a nature preserve. Many owners of weedy ponds express concern about the fate of fish and frogs during a cleanout, but most of them go ahead anyway. I admired these folks for preserving the pond that had evolved. And they'll have a good view; as close as the house is to the pond, the second-floor deck is, in effect, a pond observation platform. That's also a plus for keeping an eye on children near the pond. When my kids were young, we had a mandatory life jacket rule for trips to the pond until they became certified swimmers. Being able to keep an eye on them from the house added a margin of safety; another reason to have your pond within view from your home.

If your house is (or will be) located in the watershed above the pond, take precautions to prevent household runoff from contaminating the pond. Divert runoff from septic fields, foundation drains, fertilized gardens, and other contaminated sources away from the pond, and if the pond will be used for swimming, test the water periodically for bacterial contamination.

◄ Here is an embankment pond viewed from the dam, with the house providing a privacy buffer between the pond and the road. Like the Lornells' pond, this is landscaping with a liquid front lawn. Again, the dam is the only level land near the house.

## LANDSCAPING THE EMBANKMENT

If you do plan to build a viewing pond, make sure to discuss the size and general appearance of the dam with your contractor. As previously discussed, minimizing the artificial look of the dam structure requires good planning of principal viewpoints.

Sometimes the embankment is the only level lawn area near the pond. It has the promise to be an open space, a scenic overlook, and a garden area (only shallow-rooted plants with no fertilizer runoff, please). It can also include a beach area and a setting for stonework, sculpture, diving stones, and benches.

The shape of the embankment requires consideration. If possible, make the embankment top wide enough to accommodate the uses mentioned above. On steep slopes builders sometimes dig deep ponds that require so much excavated material that they must skimp on the dam top or import additional fill. It may be worth the extra expense, but otherwise consider lessening your depth ambitions. Try not to create unnecessary pond depth at the expense of your embankment terrace if it is the only nearby level ground.

Dams that impound water on sloping terrain have the potential to be assets. Here the builder used material from the excavation to build a wide embankment, expanding the landscape potential of the pond area. ▶

Design for freeboard (the distance between the dam top and the waterline) small enough to prevent an uninviting craterlike pond, but remember that the primary and overflow spillways must be adequate to handle peak runoff. The exterior slope must not be so steep as to be vulnerable to erosion. This is another common result of skimping on building material, especially for high dams (see illustration on page 79).

Many pond contractors prefer the flood "insurance" that comes with high freeboard, and in some situations with large watershed runoff and/or low discharge capacity, they're right. However, I prefer the benefits of modest freeboard: easy access to the water for swimming and boating, a feeling of greater intimacy with the water as you walk the shore, and a more natural appearance. Low freeboard does usually require capacious spillways: a large native spillway or discharge pipe, usually combined with an emergency spillway.

The biggest challenge to embankment landscaping is the generally accepted prohibition against trees. Tree roots are capable of breaking up the compacted embankment material enough to lead to leaks and possible dam failure. It's tough enough to build a good seepage-resistant embankment, so why add an element of structural vulnerability? Alas, a treeless site can look more like a landfill than a landscaping asset. The good news is that there are plenty of ways to enhance the appearance of your embankment short of planting trees on it.

◀ To achieve adequate pond depth and embankment height on steeply sloping terrain, dam material excavated from the basin may be in short supply. The result can be a narrow embankment with limited landscaping potential, as shown here. It may be worth importing additional fill so you don't short-change the shore area.

A foot of freeboard for this embankment sets an attractive shore height. Note how the island elevation is similar to the embankment grade, which creates a unified, natural appearance. ▶

## GRASSES AND PLANTS

If not trees, what? Lawn, for starters. That may seem obvious, but establishing a carpet of grass on heavily compacted soil can be a challenge and require patience.

Another obstacle is the ban on fertilizers, which are often used to jump-start a new lawn on disturbed soil. Fertilizers are off-limits around most ponds because of their potential to run off with rain and snow into the water and trigger unwanted algae and pond weeds. That's why pond-building plans should include a provision to reserve topsoil during site preparation. After the dam has been compacted, this soil can be reapplied to the embankment surface, making a fine medium for establishing a lawn. Once the grass has been seeded, a scattering of hay helps keep the soil from drying out or eroding before the seeds germinate. Many pond owners use a conservation mix of quick-sprouting annual grasses to quickly knit the soil together, and slower-germinating perennials.

The embankment top or back slope can be an ideal seedbed for hardy wildflowers. Wildflowers, many of which thrive in poor soils, will be easier to establish from scratch on a stripped surface before competition from weeds sets in. Contact a specialist in wildflower seeds, such as Prairie Moon Nursery, for advice on the best approach for your region and soil type. Wildflowers can also thrive on the shoreline: Here seed or plant moist-soil flowers and grasses or allow native plants to naturalize the pond margin. A wildflower border of a few feet between pond and path is plenty.

◀ The prohibition against tree planting on embankments often leaves builders with ungainly-looking dams covered with a patchy stubble of grass. It needn't be so. Here grass seed has been planted and mulched with straw to prevent erosion and encourage seeding. Topsoil saved during site clearing was reapplied during final grading to further improve soil quality on the compacted dam. In this photo landscapers in a rowboat plant shallow-rooted moist-soil shrubs around the shore. Note the compost applied along the pond perimeter, used to enhance growth without adding alga-stimulating fertilizer. Accent stones have been included for a natural look.

One simple solution to the bare-embankment syndrome is to refrain from mowing or cutting weeds along the shoreline. Allow a foot or two at the edge to naturalize, and before long you'll have a perennial border of moist-soil reeds and grasses at the shore and wildflowers and ferns farther back. ▶

Naturalized edges offer several pluses. Native plants that move in are acclimated to the area, and provide food and shelter for animals, birds, and beneficial insects like dragonflies, which feed on mosquitoes. And you won't need any fertilizer. It's a pleasure to discover and identify the variety of wildflowers that appear with the seasons. You can jump-start the process by seeding or planting your own choices.

I see many ponds—embankment and excavated—with an attractive shoreline band of black-eyed Susans, goldenrod, aquatic grasses, and more, which develop naturally. In fact, some wetland designers recommend against introducing any nursery plants or seeds, preferring to allow native plants to establish themselves. The success of these plants is almost guaranteed.

I don't limit my own pond margin to naturalized native plants alone. I especially like to see intervals of brilliant scarlet cardinal flowers—which like wet feet—along the pond edge, a pleasure I wouldn't have unless I'd introduced small plants and then scattered the mature seeds. I've also introduced various irises, daylilies, and a patch of brilliant purple lupines that have spread over the entire north shore.

◄ Increasing numbers of pond owners are aware of the benefits of naturalized shorelines. Dragonflies seem to thrive in this border area; and the more dragonflies, the fewer mosquitoes.

If your embankment includes a native spillway, the moist soils flanking the overflow channel can be another fertile area for naturalized or introduced cultivars and wildflowers. Marsh marigolds bloom in the early summer in the channel and along the edge of my own earthen spillway. I had originally planted them along the inflow stream, but they seemed to prefer the shadier spillway area, and migrated across the pond.

Small flowers and grasses along the pond edge and the spillway will not endanger your dam structure. Trees alongside the spillway can also help hold the soil together, as long as they don't compromise the dam structure. Native plants, shrubs, and mosses can also enhance the spillway. Beware, however, of introducing invasive aquatic plants. Cattails, for instance, have value as habitat and water-quality enhancers, but will spread from the pond edge into shallow areas and become a nuisance. If you allow cattails, carefully confine them to marginal areas that require regular maintenance.

Larger shallow-rooted plants can also be used on the pond embankment providing you keep them along the far edge of the dam or on the exterior backslope. I have a row of highbush

This earthen spillway at my pond is sited at the junction of the dam and the undisturbed terrain to take advantage of the erosion-resistant native soil. The marsh marigolds were originally planted at the inflow, but migrated to the shadier spillway where they blossom every spring. ▶

blueberries along the far edge of my pond embankment, as well as a couple of midsize cherry trees. The shallow-rooted blueberries and hybridized planted cherries pose no threat to the dam. Because the dam slopes up gradually from the water, the far edge is a couple of feet higher than the waterline, further reducing the chance of compromising the structure.

The blueberries and cherry trees create a privacy screen, although they are spaced with open intervals to allow a view out over the valley and distant hills. Years ago, before I planted the blueberries, I had annually planted a row of tall peas on a chicken-wire fence, which yielded privacy plus fresh vegetables. I've also seen cedars and shallow-rooted evergreen shrubs, small trees, and lilacs and roses used as privacy screens along embankment edges. Keep in mind that as fruitful as edible landscaping can be, it may also require netting or electric fencing to keep out varmints attracted to the food and the pond.

Pole structures make effective substitutes for plants and trees, and eliminate the root problem. I've seen poles with the bark still on for a pergola and trellis. The trellis, covered with flowering vines, made an elegant gateway to the pond area; the pergola, also covered with vines and featuring handmade swings and stone paving, yielded shade and screening, as well as landscaping variety on the embankment.

Many pond owners hanker for the traditional weeping willow on the shore, but willows are notorious for sending out damaging roots, and the leaves they perpetually shower in the water often lead to turbidity and an unhealthy nutrient load. (Recently I visited a pond where willows had been planted just beyond the

◀ One way to landscape your dam without compromising the structure is to put up pole structures covered with plants. This trellis and pergola were built on the pond embankment, and support climbing vines: grapes and Virginia creeper.

embankment in undisturbed soil right next to the outflow pipe, so that falling leaves are floated out of the pond by water power.)

Planting or saving trees for landscaping effect at a bit more distance is another savvy strategy, a variation on the Asian "borrowed scenery" technique, which opens up tree lines to access more distant views. Set-back trees don't cause leaf litter or root problems.

I've also seen older ponds handed down from one property owner to the next, with little attention paid to trees growing on the dam. Once a tree reaches about 6 inches at the butt, you've got a real dilemma. If you cut the tree, its roots will die and rot and possibly trigger water transmission and leaks. If you don't cut, the tree keeps growing.

In light of the prohibition against large trees, try substituting with erratic stones, stonework, and sculpture. A split-rail fence along the outside edge of the embankment is a clever way to introduce wood in lieu of actual trees. Of course, some owners prefer the uncluttered look of an unadorned embankment, which is something of a sculpture itself.

Here's a trick for taking the monotony out of an embankment's appearance. During construction of my pond, these shadbush trees were dug out of the site and replanted across the driveway, just beyond the embankment. Viewed from across the water, the trees appear to be growing on the dam. ▶

# INFLOWS AND OUTFLOWS

Embankment ponds offer more inflow and outflow design options than excavated ponds. Excavated ponds on flat terrain often preclude drains and piped spillways because there's no downslope outlet site. With the option of installing a standpipe spillway system (see "Anatomy of a Dam," page 79) and creating a seamless dam, the embankment pond builder can substitute graded terrain for an open water channel. Some people prefer a seamless embankment to an open channel. And when a driveway crosses an embankment, spillway piping is often used. Where spillway erosion is a problem piping can be a plus. If a gated drain is connected to the spillway pipe the owner can empty the pond for sediment cleanouts, repairs, vegetation control, or fish removal/harvest.

Even better, a valved drain enables the owner to drop the water level for upkeep chores without emptying the pond.

A control box spillway uses splash boards to establish the pond's water level. The boards can be removed before spring runoff to prevent flooding. Periodic removal of litter and, perhaps, beaver damming materials may be needed. Anything that gives you control of the water level will help with water quality, maintenance, and repairs.

Clearly, it's the sloping terrain home to embankment ponds that most dramatically adds to the inflow/outflow landscaping possibilities. Here native inflows and outflows can be transformed into waterfalls or cascading streams.

◄ The stones in the foreground and along the shoreline were imported to enhance the natural appearance of this embankment pond. Some areas of the embankment were built up so that large mature trees could be transplanted without causing root damage to the perimeter structure.

The dam used to create this embankment pond doubles as the driveway to the house. ►

If a stream enters and exits a pond it can usually be enhanced for appearance and erosion control with the creative use of stonework and plants. Inflow and outflow streams are variations on the same theme—running water—but there are enough differences between the two to make it worth examining them separately.

### Inflow Streams

Whether you're working with an existing pond or building a new one, be sure to find out if there are one or more inflow streams, and if so, look them over and evaluate their characteristics. Observe how much water is flowing into the pond from each. This will vary during different seasons, and it's important to observe or measure maximum stream volume. That's usually during spring runoff or fifty- to hundred-year floods, both of which can be estimated using data available from your local NRCS office. Evaluate the stream's vulnerability to erosion. The object is to determine whether the stream would bring substantial runoff into the pond, and with it high sediment loads, which in turn can fill in the pond or compromise water quality. Generally

◀ Large ponds with high discharge volume may require an engineered concrete spillway, or sluice gate, through the dam. This spillway features a trash guard to prevent damming by beavers. Removable splashboards control the pond's water level.

it's a bad idea to run a large stream directly into a pond, especially a stream with significant erosion potential. If there is potential for large stream volume, many pond owners will divert the stream around the pond, or site the pond to the side of the stream and bring in stream water, if necessary, via a bypass pipe. This sort of streamside site work may require state or federal permitting.

I've worked on several streamside ponds, and they lend themselves well to embankment construction because of the need to create a well-drained shore area in a wet site. An embankment is built between the pond and the stream, and water is piped from the stream from a pickup point upstream. In some cases the embankment may encircle the entire basin.

Perhaps you're wondering, Why build a pond if you've already got a stream? Swimming, for starters. Two of my favorite streamside ponds were built for families with kids, and swimming was a high priority for everyone. Both ponds were also stocked with trout, and each home overlooked the stream as its primary view, so digging a pond doubled the liquid assets. The ponds were built on the far side of the streams, with wood plank footbridges for access. Thus a trip to the pond also involved a trip across the stream, as a kind of visual and aural overture, and with plenty of landscaping potential in between.

At one of the ponds the path goes through several flower gardens, past a vegetable garden, and crosses the bridge onto the pond embankment, which features a large fire pit lined with handsome stones from the stream. The embankment has been extended at the upstream end to create a spacious terraced lawn. A sauna and hot tub are located close to the pond. The stream is bordered by an irregular row of tall native trees that frame the stream and pond view and create areas of privacy. Thus the home and pond suggest distinct areas. The abundance of gardens and trees balances the water energy, and the pond area has the cloistered feel of a meditation retreat.

The ideal setup for piping stream water into a pond requires a pickup point at a higher elevation than the pond. To be most efficient, the stream inlet often consists of a perforated concrete or steel structure buried at the edge of the stream, connected to the feed pipe. This prevents sediment from plugging the inlet system. The pipe can flow directly into the pond, below or above the water level. If the inflow splashes into the water, it helps oxygenate the pond. In colder climates bury the pipe below the frost line to prevent ice blockage in winter.

Stream pipes can be used to create attractive landscape features. Waterfalls of various designs can be constructed, with the stream pipe outlet at the top, cascading into the pond. Especially attractive waterfalls can be made by using a reduced and flattened fitting at the outlet to disperse the water and create a broader waterfall.

If you do have a modest stream feeding your pond directly, some erosion-control measures may be needed to prevent sedimentation. Examine the stream and entry point in the pond, looking for evidence of erosion or sedimentation in the inflow area. If the stream channel has been disturbed during construction, it may be especially susceptible to erosion.

Stone is one of the best ingredients for erosion control in streams. Industrially produced riprap or crushed stone is often used for commercial projects such as detention ponds at developments. Although this riprap has a manufactured appearance, it is easy to purchase and apply and is reasonably priced.

Before lining your stream with crushed stone you may need to excavate it a bit to create a well-defined channel. To further reduce the potential risk of erosion, install a geotextile fabric or PVC liner first.

Private pond builders and owners are likely to choose a more natural stone for stream lining. Field or quarry stone and "river" stone gathered from streams make pleasing pond inflow lines—far more natural than crushed stone. Don't forget, however, that imported "natural" stone (Pennsylvania stone, for example) may not match native rock and could look out of place as a result. I've seen Pennsylvania stone used to build waterfalls in New

◀ Inflow streams offer landscaping risks and rewards, and stone is often used to prevent erosion and to enhance visual appeal. Here native stone has been used to reinforce the streambed against erosion and for an elegant footbridge.

England, and the Band-Aid-colored stone looks jarring in a region characterized by its gray granite stone walls.

There are two basic approaches to lining streams with stone: simply fill the channel with irregular stone, or lay flat stones to create a paved effect. Again, prepare the channel with an erosion-resistant geotextile base. Make sure to bury the edges or the natural effect will be spoiled. Carelessly laid liner material almost always backfires.

Depending on the slope, inflow streams can also be modified with stone steps, or sometimes naturally rot-resistant wood, for a waterfall effect. State and federal law often require permitting for stream alterations, and no stream work should be done without checking into permit requirements.

The intermittent vein of water feeding my pond seemed to pose an erosion threat when the pond was built, so I lined the channel just above the pond with stones gathered during excavation. An attractive waterfall resulted and erosion was reduced, but over the years the channel has grown in with native grasses and the waterfall has disappeared along with the stones. And so has the erosion; with a little help nature heals itself.

Some inflow streams may best be left as is. I've seen numerous embankment ponds fed by a gently sloping stream left to meander through a wetland. Small inflows can be piped directly into the pond, allowing the builder to remove a source of pos-sible erosion and to create a uniform shore surface. For example, a gravelly upslope watershed with intermittent streams or seep springs feeding the pond may be difficult to landscape. Builders can channel these waters through belowground perforated drainage piping and into the pond. The ditches are usually back-filled with crushed stone and covered with filter fabric to prevent sediment from clogging the pipe. Thus stony, saturated, infertile ground can be transformed into a well-drained area that will often sustain trees, shrubs, and grasses. (See illustration, page 23.)

Another technique for preventing inflow-stream erosion is to dig a detention pool in the stream channel. Sometimes called silt catchment pools, these basins are located just above the main pond. Sediment flowing in the stream settles out in the detention pond, which is periodically cleaned out to make room for more settling sediment. Detention ponds can be strictly utilitarian affairs, or they can be landscaped with stonework and plants, like miniature ponds. I recently visited a pond where a detention pool had been created upstream so that its outflow cascaded down a steep stony slope into the main pond. The woods around the detention pond had been carefully preserved and combined with the waterfall to create a natural scene that offset the human-made look of the larger embankment pond.

Although detention ponds are sometimes erosion-proofed with construction fabric or PVC liners, it can be challenging to keep the edges buried and invisible, especially the upstream leading edge, which tends to become undermined. Another drawback to membrane liners is their vulnerability to damage when the silt is dredged out. One alternative is to use a structural pool of concrete, wood, or steel sunk into the stream and periodically cleaned out. Structural pools also protect intake pipes feeding downstream ponds, but they are modified to exclude silt with covers and perforations similar to well tiles.

Stonework can also be used to prevent erosion in detention ponds that receive periodically high runoff from large watersheds and/or development drainage systems. Because the water level fluctuates dramatically, large stone is installed in a wide band around the shoreline.

The detention pond approach can also apply to larger dual ponds, and sometimes the concept is reversed. I occasionally see twin ponds linked by a short spillway or stream, but it is the upper embankment pond that has the better water quality. The upper recreation pond has been constructed in a large wetland area, with the lower shallow wetland pond allowed to grow wildly and fill with sediment. Or there is a similar configuration of two ponds along a stream, with the upper pond designed for recreation and the lower for wildlife and wetland vegetation. It's a strategy also followed by fish farmers, who use a series of descending ponds, with the upper pond reserved for fish needing the best-quality water. Technically you probably can't call these upper ponds detention pools, except that they do detain good water.

I've also seen silt pools at the pond shoreline, within the pond itself. A shallow underwater berm defines the edge of the silt pool, and cattails may grow there. Thus a small wetland shelf is built into the pond, with the vegetation providing a natural wetland water filtration with root absorption. These are sometimes called speed bumps because they slow down incoming sediment.

### Outflow Streams

Outflow streams offer even more design options than inflows. You can eliminate the exposed outflow stream altogether by installing a spillway pipe. These pipes range from horizontal culvert-style

This detention pond is subject to high-volume storm-water runoff and potential erosion from fluctuating water levels. Large native stones built into vulnerable shore areas look more natural than manufactured riprap, and protect against water damage. ▶

overflow drains at pond water level (rarely recommended because of possible erosion problems) to standpipe systems that route water down and out under the embankment. The result, as mentioned earlier, is a seamless dam with no flowing water presenting obstacles to vehicles or pedestrians—and no potential for streamside landscaping either. Where culverts are installed it may be possible to cover the pipe with stonework, creating an attractive footbridge.

Pond owners use pipe overflows to ensure against erosion and flood potential, especially in large watersheds. Some couple a drain to the pipe, adding the ability to draw down or empty the pond. Often the drain is a gate controlled by a cable or rope secured to shore, or by a valve. Sometimes the drain is a separate pipe, which may or may not complement a pipe spillway. Although these piped systems can be useful, some designers and owners find them unattractive. If so they can be covered by a pier or stone. Check outlet pipes periodically to make sure that the inlet end does not become clogged with leaves or debris. A pier covering a drop inlet will often have a hatch that can be opened

for trash removal around the pipe. Trash guards are sometimes used to filter out debris. Beaver baffles may also be necessary to prevent damming activity by these great dam builders. Although many beaver baffles aren't much to look at, some specialists in "beaver deceiver" design custom-build unobtrusive devices using fence posts and sturdy wire.

Piped spillways are typically paired with an emergency spillway designed to handle overflow in excess of pipe capacity during heavy rains or snowmelt. The emergency spillway is an earthen channel in the dam that rarely flows with water. Landscaping on it is limited to grass or stone; the channel should be kept brush-free in the event it's needed.

Control structures that incorporate gated sluiceways and horizontal outflow pipes can also be used as part of a pond outlet, and they are often deployed to deter beavers.

If you don't need a piped spillway, the overflow channel can be landscaped in a way similar to that of an inflow stream. Sometimes called a native spillway, because it runs over native earth, it is often located at either end of the dam, where half the

◄ The overflow stream from a 1-acre embankment pond discharges down this natural spillway. The spillway was sited on ledge rock for erosion resistance, with some stonework used to stabilize the stream bank.

spillway base is undisturbed ground, which helps stem erosion. Running a pond overflow elsewhere across the embankment risks a higher chance of erosion and the potential for dam failure.

Locate the spillway at whichever end of the dam allows overflow to return to the original watershed stream as directly as possible. Avoid directing the outflow along the toe of the dam back to the original stream, or for any significant distance on the disturbed embankment back slope; it could undermine the embankment.

Designing an outflow stream is similar in many ways to planning a stream inflow. The object is to create something attractive and to minimize erosion. This can be done by using various types of stone, often in combination with a foundation of construction fabric or PVC liner. Pouring a layer of concrete as an erosion retardant is not recommended because it is likely to be

◄ Bridge design affects pond ambience. Wood plank bridges befit a rustic setting or wetland preserve; arched wood or iron rail bridges suggest something more formal. Consider the aesthetic effect of your bridge before installing it. ▶

undermined and eventually break up, especially if subjected to freezing and thawing.

Stonework can be casual rubble of native stone or more elaborate flat stone paving or waterfall stone steps. Native spillways also invite footbridges or heftier bridges for vehicles. Footbridge materials include fieldstone slabs, cut stone, logs, wood planks, or an elegant garden-style bridge made of wood. Your choice of bridge material can be a significant statement about your intended pond style. A bright red, arched Japanese-style garden bridge might be perfect for an Oriental teahouse pond, but you can be sure it will be jarring next to a rustic log cabin.

If fish arc stocked, place a wire mesh screen across the spillway stream to prevent fish from escaping downstream. Regularly clean the screen to prevent clogging with debris.

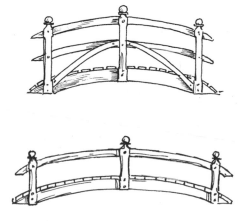

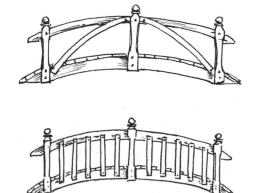

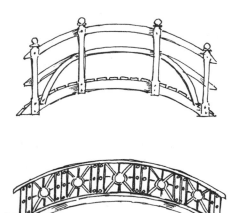

# PART FOUR

# Plants, Shrubs, and Trees

# CHAPTER SEVEN

# Save That Tree

*t*he list of possible pond and pond-side plantings is almost end-less. Your choices will depend on your taste, type of pond, existing plants, soil and water conditions, climate zone, mainte-nance obligations, and budget. Sounds a bit overwhelming, but it needn't be. There's no rush, and half the fun is taking your time to learn pond conditions and consider what you might like to try.

Regardless of pond age, site, and structure, the choices for landscaping are rich, ranging from a complete makeover to the simplest touches.

## NATIVE TREES

One of your first landscaping decisions may have nothing to do with planting at all. Instead there may be surrounding trees to preserve or cut. I've worked on several designs for ponds on wooded sites, and one of the most common questions concerned how far back the trees should be cut around the shoreline. There's no rigid formula: evaluate trees and other plantings around your pond site according to site conditions and your plans and aesthetic leanings.

Here are some landscaping strategies to consider as you size up a wooded site. There are distinct advantages to clearing at least some open space around the shore. Shoreline clearing creates open terrain, space for new plantings, reduced leaf litter, additional sunlight, and broader views. Few wooded sites will not call for some stretch of the shore to be cleared, unless the pond is dedicated exclusively to wildlife. Without some open shore you have no destination, no point of view from which to appreciate the pond. The shore may also need clearing in areas requiring drainage or fill to establish stable ground. Simply opening up shoreland to the sun helps dry out soggy terrain and allows for interesting new planting options. Open space also allows for the addition of beaches, piers, outdoor furniture, camping areas, and more.

When I built my pond one grand old yellow birch stood on the north slope directly between the house and the pond. It blocked my view of the pond, especially with its leaves deployed, and there were times I wished for a clear view of the water. But gradually the birch became a presiding spirit over the pond, with its unique short trunk and symmetrical bouquet of branches. Genius loci, living sculpture, dragoman of weather and seasons, the tree was the head of the pond, figuratively and literally.

After two decades the tips of the branches began to die. And year after year the tree decayed. Skeletal limbs evoked year-round winter. Death. Branches cracked and fell, often hanging up in the crown. But like the birch, I hung on, justifying its wildlife value as a snag and as a revered member of the family. The kids still swung from one of the branches, flying over the water. Would it hold? I couldn't bear to watch anymore. It was like having an old pet limping around the house in brave agony.

I cut the tree and bucked it up for firewood, which completed a circle of some kind. And the view? Now I see the entire pond, unobstructed, and what were once two distinct regions separated by a single tree are now one, and a less interesting one at that. There's a loss of mystery or spirit, the ineffable element that nature occasionally blesses on a special landscape. Sometimes, briefly, I see the tree again, guarding over the pond. So of course it's not gone, not really.

Still, it's a great puzzle what to do with the space. I've thought of planting another tree, for my children's generation. Perhaps build a pergola. Maybe both. The lesson of the yellow birch? The landscaping effect of even a single tree can be enormous. I'm sure glad I didn't cut that tree in the initial excitement of site clearing.

## SAVING, THINNING, OR REMOVING

If your house will overlook your pond and there are trees between the two, consider thinning but not removing the trees. Keeping a few trees between house and pond can establish a sense of separation and privacy for both locations. If the trees are hardwoods, enjoy the dramatic scene change in fall, when the leaves drop and a window on the pond is suddenly opened. (See photograph, page 6.)

Saving selected native trees offers more practical benefits, especially considering the price, growing time, care (especially watering and pest protection), and uncertain outcome of nursery purchases. In wet areas that might be vulnerable to erosion, existing trees help stabilize the terrain. This is often the case on slopes uphill from embankment ponds. Although higher groundwater levels created by a new pond may kill shoreline trees, you'll never know unless you try preserving one. Ponds with earthen inflows and/or spillways often benefit from trees bordering the channel to prevent erosion.

The wildlife benefits of trees are well known. In general, trees afford habitat and food. Birds attracted to trees may reward you by keeping the insect population down. Even a dead tree may be worth saving. Snags are usually full of insects and nesting potential. In Victorian England dead trees were saved (sometimes even imported) on country estates where a Gothic atmosphere was desired. However, trees provide sniper positions for predatory birds like kingfishers; if you plan on raising fish, you may look at shoreline trees suspiciously.

Flowering trees are worth saving for their fruit and spring blossoms. I saved a couple of old apple trees around my pond, and the effect every spring is dazzling, with bright blossoms reflected on the water. When the blossoms drop they cover the water like confetti. During construction we were also able to dig up several shadbush on the site and replant them just beyond the dam. I've watched them blossom every spring for more than twenty years.

Most ponds benefit from at least one good shade tree, and all the better if yours already exists. Keep an eye out for a tree close to the shore and that has a sturdy branch for a rope swing. For years we had the yellow birch with a swing for the kids, and it gave them a fairway ride overlooking the water. And if you're lucky you might find a tree branch on a shoreline on which to hang a rope for Tarzan-style swoops into the water.

Before you cut consider the visual qualities of existing trees around the pond. Sugar maple and red maple leaves flame up in fall. White birch trunks contrast dramatically with surrounding greenery and create impressionistic rippling reflections. Conifers have a year-round sculptural presence and become bewitching when covered by a fall of snow.

All adjacent trees should be evaluated for their buffering potential. As wind, sound, and privacy screens, the right trees in the right place can be invaluable—especially conifers. If your pond is near your property line it's doubly important to consider the screening potential of existing trees, whether you need them now or not. You never know who will move in next door.

Ponds often wind up sited near neighboring property, especially in hill country, where maximum runoff may gather at the bottom of a slope near a borderline. For example, my pond is close to the property line, and for many years the neighbor's land was thick woods. Nevertheless I maintained a buffer of trees on my side, just in case. Last year, the property changed hands, the trees were cut, and the house enlarged. My tree line preserved my privacy. In effect, doing nothing was one of the best landscaping decisions I ever made.

There are situations when it may pay to clear a wide margin around the pond. Otherwise beavers might be attracted to a stand of appetizing hardwoods (poplar, alder, white birch), although it usually makes sense to wait until trouble develops before cutting. If leaf litter becomes a problem, clearing may also be necessary.

Removing trees from the watershed can release water to the site if supply is short. Runoff to the pond will be affected by forestation in the watershed, and the fewer trees you have wicking up water above the site, the more water will be available to the pond. For several years after construction of my pond the water did not reach overflow level during the summer season, when fresh exchange is essential to water quality. Transforming the woods above the pond into a meadow released enough runoff to fill the pond. Keep in mind that cutting should always be accompanied by provisions for erosion control due to stumping, topsoil disturbance by machinery, and trail or road building. Fortunately, the trees above my pond were not the same ones I needed as a privacy buffer.

A good rule of thumb is to survey your adjacent trees and imagine how the place would look and function without them. Consider the potential for privacy and sound barriers, landscaping effects, leaf litter, and other issues. When in doubt hold the ax! You can always cut later. Flag all protected trees before clearing and construction begins, and be especially careful not to backfill material around the tree trunks, which can kill the tree.

When removing trees from the pond site itself be sure to remove the stumps as well. Perimeter cutting may also benefit from stumping, especially where a graded lawn or field will be created. Yet stumping may add significantly to the cost and require additional erosion control, especially on slopes. It's not always necessary, especially in wooded areas. In wetland areas stumping may require a permit from your state DNR and/or the U.S. Army Corps of Engineers.

Disposal of stumps can be accomplished by burial on the property, bearing in mind that you should never bury stumps in the main structure of a dam. Even in the dam back slope or around an excavated pond shore, rotting stumps can lead to slumping and uneven grades. Stumps, and any organic matter buried around the pond, can also decay and cause off-color water.

# CHAPTER EIGHT

# *Planting Considerations and Techniques*

## SOIL, SUN, AND CLIMATE

*b*efore buying any seeds, plants, shrubs, or trees, familiarize yourself with water quality and the soil conditions around the perimeter of your pond. Terrestrial plants have varying soil requirements, and water and soil quality can affect aquatic species.

The terrain around a pond will often vary widely in moisture content and soil quality. In the space of a few yards the soil might range from a highly compacted gravelly embankment to a rich loamy edge or submerged mud.

Soil borings or some shoveling will help gauge soil quality and groundwater level; while you're at it, testing different areas for pH is also useful.

Make a sketch of the pond and the surrounding terrain to be landscaped, noting soil condition, pH, and the sunlight/shade factor. Clay, peaty soil, loams, and sands and gravels have differing influences on a variety of plants. Knowing your soils will help you select plants and trees that are likely to succeed. When choosing plants, match their soil requirements with the corresponding terrain. Many plants can succeed in a variety of soil conditions; others are more particular.

Soils can sometimes be modified to suit a particular plant's requirements. Be especially careful, however, about increasing fertility with nutrients that can wash into the pond and trigger algal and aquatic-weed problems. Note areas that may be subject to periodic flooding, which various plant and tree species may or may not tolerate.

The highly compacted gravelly embankment at my pond was by no means an ideal planting medium. So I dug trenches and holes, and refilled with fertile garden soil to establish areas for a pea fence, blueberries, and hybrid cherry trees. These areas were located at the far edge of the embankment to prevent any garden nutrients from washing into the pond and adversely affecting water quality.

It's also important to classify areas in terms of available sunlight and plant hardiness zone. Various plants and trees respond differently to shade and sun, and plant catalogs state sunlight requirements. You can find your hardiness zone on gardening maps, but variations in terrain and exposure can affect classification. For example, my pond lies in a hollow that gets little sun from fall to spring, and a lot of north wind and blowing snow. According to garden maps I'm in Zone Four, but to be safe, at the pond I plant only varieties suitable for Zone Three.

## FIRST PLANTINGS AROUND A NEW POND

After construction of the pond, your first task is to stabilize exposed soil. Use a conservation seed mix that combines a quick-sprouting annual grass with deeper-rooted perennials that take longer to establish. The shoreland around the pond is likely to have been heavily compacted during construction and may contain a high percentage of clay, which is not especially conducive to plant growth. That's why the building process often begins with stripping and saving topsoil from the site, which is spread around the pond in the final stage.

Use a protective mulch of hay to prevent the topsoil and grass seed from eroding during rainfall. Because hay can also contribute weed seeds, some builders prefer to mulch with seedless straw or a biodegradable mesh fabric. Hay or fabric is especially useful on dam banks and other bare soil slopes.

Native wildflowers are another option for ground cover at this stage. It's rare to have such a large spread of bare soil, ripe for establishing a new plant regime, and why not natives? They give you the chance to help reestablish indigenous plant communities; they are more appropriate to the setting than their cultivated, hybridized relatives; and as long as you select the right ones, they are perfectly adapted.

Overcoming native weeds and grasses is one of the major challenges in establishing wildflower fields. Even freshly stripped or turned-over shoreland soil contains vigorous, long-lasting weed seeds, and considerable effort is usually required to dispatch them and make room for selected wildflowers. Mulching, using cover crops, burning, and tilling are some of the techniques used to prepare for wildflower planting.

The dam slope is an area that may benefit dramatically from wildflowers. Embankment slopes can look artificial and bulky, even with a grass cover, and they are difficult to mow. Wildflowers are an attractive alternative, a cascade of color and texture to transform a monotonous green buttress into a living tapestry that changes colors through the seasons and, once established, requires little maintenance. The embankment top is another good candidate for wildflowers. Not only do the flowers provide a dazzling array of colors, but many of them attract butterflies and hummingbirds, and because they are not mowed, they discourage Canada geese. Contact a nursery specializing in wildflowers to discuss various species suited to your region and growing conditions, as well as preparations for seeding. Some wildflower seed mixes include the grasses you initially need to hold your soil together, as well as the flowers, which are slower to become established.

Plant trees or shrubs after a good grass or wildflower cover is established, to protect against erosion and retain moisture. Remember, planting trees (or allowing trees to grow) on a dam may threaten embankment integrity.

New plantings are more vulnerable to temperature extremes and heavy rainfall than established ones, and need special attention.

Planting is most likely to succeed in moist soils. Watering may be necessary. Other factors affecting success include planting season, amount of sunlight, and climate zone. Be sure to match new plantings with these local conditions.

## SELECTING AND SITING TREES

Planning for trees requires an assessment of the soil around your pond. Evaluate soil texture (sand/gravel, silt, clay) and pH, as well as moisture content and groundwater level. Once you've mapped the soil around your pond you'll be able to do a better job of matching tree species to a specific area.

As you begin to consider tree species, you'll need to match their climate, sunlight, and soil preferences to your site. Keep in mind that many trees can adapt to a variety of conditions, and different varieties within one species may best suit your conditions.

To easily and reliably judge your site's potential for trees, simply look around the neighborhood. Trees that appear to thrive in your region are good candidates. Native species should be given primary attention; with the exception of trees plagued by recent exotic blights, natives are most likely to succeed.

Living in a forested area of Vermont, I'm surrounded by healthy species of both conifers and hardwood deciduous trees. When I built my pond, I saved numerous trees on the slope above the pond, then gradually thinned them to include hemlocks, spruce and balsam fir, white birch and oak, native apple trees, and, as I described earlier, the monumental old yellow birch overlooking the pond. The conifers provide sound and visual screening along the property line. The three white birches are clustered like a big bouquet. And the springtime apple blossoms contrast brightly with the predominant greenery, while the fruits attract deer and other wildlife. Because of the abundance of existing trees on the watershed slope, I never had a need for nursery imports in that area.

The new embankment, however, was bare. After a trip to the local nursery I planted blueberry bushes and a couple of native pin cherry trees on the outside edge of the dam. When I remember to put out the netting, the shrubs usually yield abundant fruit.

Whether you're planning to add small trees on an embankment or larger species upslope or around an excavated pond, imagine how the trees will look over time as they grow and, in the case of deciduous trees, leaf out, change color in autumn, and shed their leaves. The bare limb structure of some trees is more attractive than others.

Large trees appeal to many, which is why people buy fast-growing species like ash and birch. Be aware, however, that fast growers are often relatively short-lived. If you're in for the long haul, consider long-lived species like maple and oak. Whichever you choose, imagine your trees reaching full size so that you get a sense of how they might block a good view or crowd another tree. As your trees grow and become leafy, will they create desirable shade or perhaps shade out plants or a garden that needs sunlight?

I've often noted that ponds surrounded by pine trees display off-color water. It's a brown tealike hue, which may be due to tannins leaching out of the trees. Although nontoxic, it's not an effect I'd choose. One or two white pines around the shore probably won't alter water quality, but I'd be cautious about planting in large numbers.

Point of view is important when choosing what and where to plant. If you'll be spending most of your time at the pond in one particular area, pay attention to the view. Are there one or more trees that you might like to keep, whether a mature species or a sapling with growth potential? Be sure to protect and tag keepers before construction begins.

If the view suggests the need for planting, take your time choosing. Consider the length of time you're willing to wait for a tree to reach desirable size. It is possible to buy large mature trees for planting, but they are expensive to purchase and plant and may require special care, including support cables and watering. Smaller starter saplings are more practical.

## TREE SPECIES

The following species are likely to do well in the moist soils around ponds. To maximize your chances for success, evaluate your climate zone, sunlight availability, and soil, and research species requirements before planting.

Alder

Birch, white or yellow

Box elder

Cedar

Cypress

Elm

Gum

Hackberry

Magnolia

Maple, red or silver

Oak poplar

Shadbush (serviceberry)

Sycamore

Viburnum

Weeping willow

White ash

White pine

## AQUATIC AND SHORELAND PLANTS

Ponds offer the unique opportunity to "landscape" with water-loving plants. Their habitat profile ranges from moist-soil areas near the edge to shoreline shallows, and finally deeper areas that are home to both emergent and submergent plants.

Moist-soil and aquatic plants offer both aesthetic and functional benefits. Cattails, rushes, *Eupatorium*, iris, cardinal flower, marsh marigold, and dozens more can yield dramatic decorative qualities. These and other varieties can contribute to water-quality improvement, erosion control, wildlife habitat, and flood mitigation.

Today the functional benefits of native aquatics are commonly recognized and supported by federal and state wetland protection laws. Additionally, across the country and the world wetlands are being constructed for their environmental benefits. Aquatic plants like cattails and rushes serve as the filters in natural wastewater-treatment wetlands. Their capacity to absorb pollutants, sponge up water, and stabilize soil also qualifies them for use in detention ponds designed to buffer watershed runoff and storm-water drainage.

Aquatic plants are, in turn, affected by water quality: clarity, pH, nutrients, oxygen, and so on. So check your water chemistry before planting. Turbid water can, for example, cut off sunlight and halt photosynthesis in submerged plants, while floating-leaved plants like water lilies aren't bothered.

Falling water levels can weaken wetland plants, but many plants (cattails, rushes) are quite tough and withstand moderate drought.

Aquatic plants will be affected by depth. Wetland plant catalogs usually feature cross-sectional diagrams of pond edges, showing which plants are suited to various depths.

Wetland plants can succeed in a variety of soils, but be alert for peat soils and for clays and gravels, which lack nutrients and discourage root development.

◀ Pond plants vary in their moisture requirements, from moist-soil edge varieties to shallow-water emergents and submergent species.

## PLANT CHECKLIST

- Is a plant annual or perennial? Obviously, annuals are likely to need replacing every year.
- Is the plant persistent or not? The stalks of persistent plants, like cattails, stand up throughout the year. Wildlife habitat and food, as well as erosion control, are often benefits of persistent plants. Nonpersistent plants (water lilies, smaller aquatics) generally die off in winter.
- Familiarize yourself with a plant's growth rate and how it spreads—by root system, seed, plant fragments, or in clumps.
- When you purchase a plant, find out what kind of plant material you'll be dealing with—seed, rootstock, tuber, bulb, or potted plant.
- Learn what area of the country the plant grows in to make sure it suits your hardiness zone; also make sure your site will fulfill a plant's sunlight requirements.
- Does the plant variety require a male and female plant to reproduce?
- Learn about the plant's appearance—height, flower color, fruit color, and drip-line perimeter.
- What are the wildlife benefits? Drawbacks? Are you likely to have problems with predators like deer, beaver, or muskrat?
- A plant's water requirements can range from intermittent moist soil to submersion. Is it able to tolerate flooding, and for how long? Be sure your habitat meets the plant's requirements.

## PLANTER BEWARE

For all the benefits of aquatic plants, many have Jekyll and Hyde personalities. Whether intentionally introduced or naturally seeded, they look fine in controlled quantities, but they may also spread and threaten to colonize an entire pond.

Pond depth is a factor in a plant's invasiveness. Many aquatic plants thrive in relatively shallow areas and stop multiplying in depths greater than 3 or 4 feet. That's why ponds are often designed with basins featuring shallow-water shoreline shelves for aquatics, which then drop off steeply to discourage invasiveness. Manual control (weeding) may be necessary to confine plants.

Correct pond design can also help discourage the spread of invasive aquatic weeds and algae. Good depth, proper slopes, and an adequate new-water exchange help deter aquatic weeds. Alas, aggressive exotic invasives like Eurasian milfoil can grow in deep water and may require manual removal, bottom barriers, or, worst of all, chemical herbicide. Make sure any plants you buy are uncontaminated by other species. Some wetland nurseries are state-regulated and the plants are certified weed-free.

Familiarize yourself with basic plant characteristics as you plan your pondscape. Determine whether a plant is invasive and, if so, to what degree. Usually the larger the plant (cattails, rushes), the slower it spreads. A plant that spreads by its root system will expand its territory more slowly than one that spreads by seed. To prevent spreading, some water gardeners contain decorative invasives in submerged pots, which can be removed at the end of the season. To control stands of larger plants like cattails, manual removal may be required. Bottom barriers can also be installed to prevent expansive rooting.

## PLANTING STRATEGIES

When I work with prospective pond builders, I recommend that they visit other ponds to help them visualize design elements and get a feel for the variety of ways that ponds can fit into the environment. The same goes for landscaping. Pond owners and builders often express an interest in "doing something landscape-wise," but they're not exactly sure what. You can learn a lot by looking at other ponds. If you see an interesting pond from the road, pull over and take a closer look. Visit ponds in your neighborhood. Analyze what you see; take notes and pictures. Ask yourself, What makes this pond attractive—the shape of the basin, relationship to the house or surrounding terrain, plantings, stonework, inflows and outflows, bridges, outbuildings?

It's striking how many attractive ponds feature minimal aquatic landscaping. In fact, I don't often see true aquatics introduced into large ponds. Why? Because most pond owners know, or have learned from experience, that just about all aquatic plants are invasive; they don't want plants colonizing the water. The aquatic plants that are present have usually naturalized on their own: cattails, water lilies, rushes, and reeds. Interest in those plants is likely to be in cutting them back, keeping them under control, or eliminating them outright.

Another reason that pond owners are likely to eschew adding aquatic plants is their potential for attracting pond pests, especially muskrats. Besides eating the plants and using them for habitat, muskrats attracted to a pond are liable to dig holes around the shoreline that can lead to structural damage and possibly leakage, especially in dams.

It's also true that some plants, shrubs, and trees suited to terrain set back from the shoreline attract nuisance animals, most prominently beaver and deer. (At the end of chapter 9 you'll find a list of plants unattractive to deer.) Like muskrat, beaver have the potential to damage the pond structure; deer are limited to damaging plants and trees, and possibly puncturing a membrane pond liner.

Despite these caveats, many pond owners do plant their ponds, and I find that a significant percentage of them hire gardeners to do the work for them. Gardening can require a lot of work and horticultural savvy. Don't rule out outsourcing your landscape work, perhaps to help plan and establish an initial design and then for periodic upkeep. I know many pond owners who hire landscape gardeners so they can work and learn alongside them.

The plant fundamentals in chapter 9 should help you select and arrange plantings. As we've seen, there are entire categories of plants suited to ponds: the true aquatics, which may be submerged or partially submerged (water lilies, cattails, arrowroot); the damp-feet plants (reeds, sedges); and the moist-soil plants (irises, cardinal flowers, ferns).

Familiarize yourself with the plants in each category; what they look like throughout the season, climate zone and soil preferences, and so on. Just as important, keep in mind that standard gardening practice places larger plants in back of a viewing area, with successively smaller ones in front. When applied to ponds, this strategy suggests that smaller plants would be aquatics, midsize would be damp-feet, and the largest would be moist-soil, as you move back from the shoreline.

You might have marsh marigolds at the shoreline with a backdrop of ferns. Sweet flag or cardinal flower is often a good choice between shoreline aquatics and more distant plants. A mass of tall, moisture-tolerant perennials works well near the shore, and tall aquatic plants such as cattails and reeds provide screening.

Landscape gardeners working in moist soils and shorelines are in general agreement about certain favorite plants. Joe-pye weed (*Eupatorium*) and queen of the prairie are two flowering perennials often suggested as backdrop plants or for screening, and unlike aquatics they are not invasive. Moist-soil phlox, rudbeckia (black-eyed Susan), lily, trollius, iris, and lobelia are among the well-esteemed midsize flowering plants. Favored shorter flowering plants include astilbe, marsh marigold, trillium, and Jacob's ladder. Acquaint yourself with the different flowering plants as you plan your pond garden.

Foliage plants are another valued ingredient of many pond gardens; they provide variety, balance, accent, and framing. These include many ferns, sedges, grasses, and rushes, as well as cattails and wild rice. Some have flowers (usually quite small); some don't. Among the well-regarded grasses are fowl meadow grass, mana grass, and ribbon grass. Different ferns are adapted to various levels of soil saturation. Among suggested varieties are ostrich, marsh, and sensitive ferns. Cinnamon fern and royal fern, two sun-tolerant ferns, are also pond-side favorites. Again, familiarize yourself with each plant's characteristics, and beware of invasive varieties.

# CHAPTER NINE

# Recommended Pond Plants

*M*ore than in a garden or greenhouse, plants in and around a pond seem to shine their brightest. Bathed in reflected light from the water below as well as overhead sun, doubled in mass by liquid mirroring, and strikingly vibrant because of their rich liquid diet, a perimeter of plants around water is a planter's rainbow.

The following plants all represent potential embellishments for your pond. The photos can help you identify existing plants as well as potential acquisitions; many of these varieties establish themselves naturally as native species. Species native to your region will grow best, without displacing other natives.

Before you begin planting, acquaint yourself with specific plant characteristics and growth requirements. There are many fine reference books available, and even more enlightening are the living examples to be found at public botanical gardens—and perhaps the pond next door.

## MOIST-SOIL PLANTS AND SHRUBS

Ajuga

Arrowhead

Arum

Astilbe

Black cohosh

Blazing star

## MOIST-SOIL PLANTS AND SHRUBS

Buttonbush

Calla lily

Cardinal flower

Culver's root

Frog fruit

Gentian

## MOIST-SOIL PLANTS AND SHRUBS

Goatsbeard

Highbush blueberry

Iris

Jack-in-the-pulpit

Jacob's ladder

Joe-pye weed

## MOIST-SOIL PLANTS AND SHRUBS

Ligularia

Lily

Lizard's tail

Marsh marigold

Meadow rue

Phlox

## MOIST-SOIL PLANTS AND SHRUBS

Physostegia

Pickerelweed

Queen of the prairie

Rose mallow

Rudbeckia

Skunk cabbage

## MOIST-SOIL PLANTS AND SHRUBS

Swamp milkweed

Sweet flag

Sweet pepperbush

Trillium

Turtlehead

Virginia sweetspire

## MOIST-SOIL PLANTS AND SHRUBS

## SEDGES, GRASSES, AND FERNS

Water avens

Cinnamon fern

Common rush

Mana grass

Ribbon grass

## SEDGES, GRASSES, AND FERNS

## AQUATIC PLANTS

Royal fern

Sensitive fern

Arrowhead

Tufted-hair grass

Bulrush

Bur reed

Cattail

Coontail

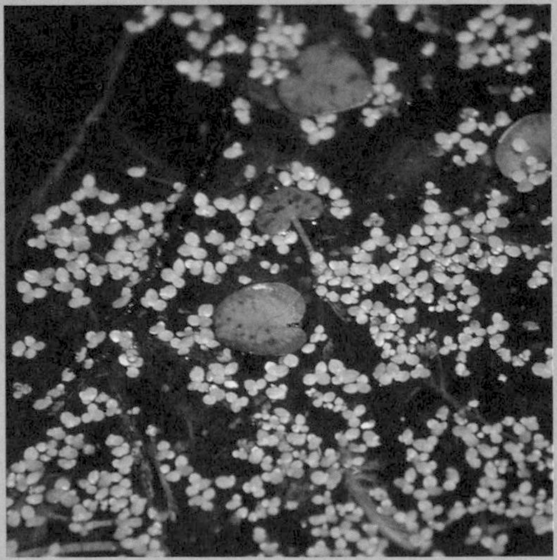

Duckweed

Elodea

Pickerel plant

## AQUATIC PLANTS

Sago pondweed

Smartweed

Watercress

Water lily

Wild rice

## DEER-RESISTANT PLANTS

Achillea*

Allium*

Artemisia

Aster

Astilbe

Campanula

## DEER-RESISTANT PLANTS

Centaurea

Chrysanthemum

Clematis

Coreopsis

Delphinium

Digitalis

## DEER-RESISTANT PLANTS

Echinacea

Epimedium

Geranium

Helleborus

Iris

Lamium

## DEER-RESISTANT PLANTS

Lupinus

Monarda

Myosotis

Nepeta*

Origanum

Paeonia

## DEER-RESISTANT PLANTS

Penstemon

Perovskia

*Phlox subulata*

Pulmonaria

Rudbeckia

Salvia*

## DEER-RESISTANT PLANTS

Sedum

Stachys

Veronica

\*Repels deer

# RESOURCES

## BOOKS & OTHER PUBLICATIONS

*Aquaculture* **Magazine**
P.O. Box 2329
Asheville, NC 28802
828-254-7334
www.aquaculturemag.com
*Excellent trade magazine with extremely useful buyer's guide, especially fish hatchery section.*

**Aquatic Bookshop**
P.O. Box 2150
Shingle Springs, CA 95682-2150
530-622-7547
www.seahorses.com
*Mail-order bookstore specializing in garden ponds and aquaculture. Extensive book list available.*

*Build a Pond for Food and Fun*
By D.J. Young
Bulletin A-19
Storey Publishing
210 MASS MoCA Way
North Adams, MA 01247
800-441-5700
www.storey.com

*Building Waterfalls, Pools, and Streams*
By Richard M. Koogle and Charles B.
Thomas
Ortho Guides
*Available from Lilypons Water Gardens
(listed separately).*

*The Complete Pond Builder: Creating a
Beautiful Water Garden*
By Helen Nash
Sterling Publishing Co., Inc.
387 Park Avenue South
New York, NY 10016
800-367-9692
www.sterlingpub.com

*Cottage Water Systems*
By Max Burns
Cottage Life Books
54 St. Patrick Street
Toronto, Ontario M5T 1V1
Canada
416-599-2000
www.cottagelife.com

*Create Your Own Water Garden*
By Charles B. Thomas
Storey Publishing
210 MASS MoCA Way
North Adams, MA 01247
800-441-5700
www.storey.com
*Pamphlet.*

*Creating Fresh Water Wetlands*
By Donald Hammer
CRC Press, Inc.
2000 Corporate Boulevard, NW
Boca Raton, FL 33431
800-272-7737
www.crcpress.com
*Thorough text by wetland expert.
Recommended.*

*The Divining Hand*
By Christopher Bird
Whitford Press
Schiffer Publishing
4880 Lower Valley Road
Atglen, PA 19310
610-593-1770
www.schifferbooks.com
*A history and how-to of dowsing for water
(and other resources). Classic book, fasci-
nating subject.*

*Earth Ponds: The Country Pond Maker's
Guide to Building, Maintenance, and
Restoration* and *Earth Ponds A to Z: An
Illustrated Encyclopedia*
By Tim Matson
The Countryman Press
P.O. Box 748
Woodstock, VT 05091
800-233-4830
*www.countrymanpress.com*

*Farm Pond Harvest* Magazine
1390 North 14500 East Road
Momence, IL 60954
815-472-2686
www.farmpondmagazine.com
*Good source of information on pond construc-
tion, maintenance and fish stocking; useful
ads. Quarterly.*

*Garden Design* Magazine
460 N. Orlando Avenue, Suite 200
Winter Park, FL 32789
800-513-0848
www.gardendesignmag.com

*Gardening with Water*
By James Van Sweden
Random House
*Excellent water-gardening guide; out of
print; check libraries or Internet.*

*Gazebos and Other Outdoor Structures* and
*Quick Guide: Gazebo*
Creative Homeowner Press
www.creativehomeowner.com
*Out of print; check libraries or Internet.*

*How to Identify Water Weeds and Algae: A
Guide to Water Management*
Cygnet Enterprises, Inc.
1860 Bagwell Street
Flint, MI 48503
800-359-7531
www.cygnetenterprises.com

*Japanese Gardens*
By Bring and Wayembergh
McGraw Hill Co.
*Excellent coverage of history and layout of Kyoto gardens. Out of print; check libraries or Internet.*

*Landscaping for Wildlife*
By Carrol L. Henderson
Minnesota Department of Natural Resources
Minnesota's Bookstore
660 Olive Street
St. Paul, MN 55155
800-657-3757
www.comm.media.state.mn.us/bookstore
*A thorough, beautifully illustrated guide to creating habitat for all sorts of wildlife, including waterfowl. While the focus is on animals and plants native to the northern Midwest, the principles apply around the country. Order from Minnesota's bookstore, address above.*

*Lake and Pond Management Guidebook*
By Steve McComas
Lewis Publishers
2000 Corporate Boulevard
Boca Raton, FL 33431
800-272-7737
www.crcpress.com
*Updated and expanded version of* Lake Smarts, *the excellent pond management guide. Recommended.*

*Land and Water* Magazine
P.O. Box 1197
Fort Dodge, IA 50501
515-576-3191
www.landandwater.com
*Essential reading for pond designers and contractors; a goldmine of building and maintenance strategies; business and government references; excellent annual Buyer's Guide; solid information on the latest techniques in water management and aquatic landscaping.*

*Native Vegetation for Lakeshores, Stream Sides, and Wetland Buffers*
Vermont Agency of Natural Resources
Water Quality Division
103 South Main Street
Waterbury, VT 05671-0408
802-241-3770
www.vtwaterquality.org
*How to establish shoreline trees, shrubs, and plants to provide cover and food for wildlife. Planting techniques and species suggestions. A good illustrated guidebook for Vermont, and also of value throughout much of the Northeast. (Beware foliage fallout and roots in embankments!)*

*Pond Boss* Magazine
P.O. Box 12
Sadler, TX 76264
903-564-6144
www.pondboss.com
*New magazine that keeps getting better, with good information, resources, and a sense of humor to boot. Worth a look.*

*Pondkeeper* Magazine
1000 Whitetail Court
Duncansville, PA 16635
814-695-4325
www.pondkeeper.com
*Excellent array of articles, products, and ads. Aimed at the wholesale trade market, but worth a look for ideas and leads.*

*The Pond Doctor*
By Helen Nash
Sterling Publishing Co., Inc.
387 Park Avenue South
New York, NY 10016
800-367-9692
www.sterlingpub.com

*Ponds: Planning, Design, Construction*
Handbook 590
U.S. Department of Agriculture
Natural Resources Conservation Service
14th Street and Independence Avenue, SW
P.O. Box 2890
Washington, DC 20013
202-720-3210
www.nrcs.usda.gov
*Excellent construction guide. Try your local NRCS office for a copy; otherwise go to the NRCS website and search for the title, which can be downloaded.*

*The Sauna*
By Rob Roy
Chelsea Green Publishing Co.
P.O. Box 428
White River Junction, VT 05001
800-639-4099
www.chelseagreen.com

*Sheds: The Do It Yourself Guide for the Backyard Builder*
By David Stiles
Firefly Books
3680 Victoria Park Avenue
Willowdale, Ontario M2H 3K1
Canada
800-387-5085
www.fireflybooks.com

*Stonescaping: A Guide to Using Stone in Your Garden*
By Jan Kowalczewski Whitner
Storey Publishing
210 MASS MoCA Way
North Adams, MA 01247
800-441-5700
www.storey.com
*Good book on stonework including its use in and around garden ponds.*

*Tim Matson's Earth Ponds Video*
Earth Ponds
288 Miller Pond Road
Thetford Center, VT 05075
802-333-9019
www.earthponds.com
*Books, videos, consulting services, and illustrated reports on pond construction and repair projects.*

*Water Features for Small Gardens*
By Francesca Greenoak
Trafalgar Square Publishing
*Out of print; check libraries or the Internet.*

*Water Gardening for Plants and Fish*
By Charles B. Thomas
T.F.H. Publications
*Available from Lilypons Water Gardens (listed separately).*

*Water Gardening* Magazine
P.O. Box 607
St. John, IN 46373
219-374-9419
www.watergardening.com
*Excellent source of ideas and materials.*

*Water Gardening: Water Lilies and Lotuses*
By Perry D. Slocum and Peter Robinson
Timber Press
*Considered by many garden experts to be the most complete book on water lilies and lotuses, written by two of the world's leading water-gardening experts. Covers water garden design, construction, maintenance, and plants. Out of print; check libraries or the Internet.*

*Water Gardens*
By Charles Thomas and Jacqueline Heriteau
Houghton Mifflin
222 Berkeley Street
Boston, MA 02116
800-225-3362
www.houghtonmifflinbooks.com

*Water Gardens: A Harrowsmith Gardener's Guide*
Edited by David Archibald and Mary Patton
Firefly Books
3680 Victoria Park Avenue
Willowdale, Ontario M2H 3K1
Canada
800-387-5085
www.fireflybooks.com

*Water Gardens: How to Plan and Plant a Backyard Pond*
By Charles B. Thomas
Taylor's Weekend Gardening Guides
Houghton Mifflin
222 Berkeley Street
Boston, MA 02116
800-225-3362
www.houghtonmifflinbooks.com

*Water in the Garden*
By James Allison
Little, Brown & Company
*Out of print; check libraries or the Internet.*

*Waterscaping*
By Judy Glattstein
Storey Publishing
210 MASS MoCA Way
North Adams, MA 01247
800-441-5700
www.storey.com
*A superior all-around guide to water gardening, with plenty of information on plants for natural ponds, including historical background and design schemes.*

*Waterside Planting*
By Philip Swindells
Sterling Publishing Co., Inc.
*Out of print; check libraries or the Internet.*

*Wetland Planting Guide for the Northeastern United States*
By Gwendolyn A. Thunhorst
Environmental Concern, Inc.
201 Boundary Lane
P.O. Box P
St. Michaels, MD 21663
410-745-9620
www.wetland.org
*Comprehensive guide to plants for wetland creation, restoration, and enhancement. Includes details on wildlife benefits, planting suggestions, and drawings. Excellent.*

## TOPOGRAPHIC MAPS

**U.S. Geological Survey**
Department of the Interior
National Center
Reston, VA 22029
888-ASK-USGS (275-8747)
store.usgs.gov

**Timely Discount Topos**
9769 West 119th Drive
Suite 9
Broomfield, CO 80020
800-821-1609
www.usgstopomaps.com

## PRODUCTS & SUPPLIERS

The following aquacultural suppliers offer a variety of products, including aeration equipment, pumps, water conditioners, and piping.

**Aquacenter, Inc.**
166 Seven Oakes Road
Leland, MS 38756
800-748-8921
www.aquacenterinc.com

**Aquatic Eco-Systems, Inc.**
1767 Benbow Court
Apopka, FL 32703
800-422-3939
www.aquaticeco.com

**Eagar, Inc.**
P.O. Box 540476
North Salt Lake, UT 84054
800-423-6249
www.eagarinc.com

**Lehman's**
P.O. Box 41
Kidron, OH 44636
888-438-5343
www.lehmans.com

**Malibu Water Resources**
P.O. Box 20928
Oxnard, CA 93033
800-490-9170
www.malibuwater.com

**O'Brock Windmills**
9435 12th Street
North Benton, OH 44449
330-584-4681
www.obrockwindmills.com

**Otterbine Barebo, Inc.**
3840 Main Road East
Emmaus, PA 18049
800-237-8837
www.otterbine.com

**Stoney Creek Equipment Co.**
11073 Peach Avenue
Grant, MI 49327
800-448-3873
www.stoneycreekequip.com

## AERATION EQUIPMENT

**Air-O-Lator**
8100 Paseo
Kansas City, MO 64131
800-821-3177
www.airolator.com

**The Power House, Inc.**
20 Gwynns Mill Court
Owing Mills, MD 21117
800-243-4741
www.thepowerhouseinc.com

**Vertex Water Features**
426 Southwest 12th Avenue
Deerfield, FL 33442
800-432-4302
www.vertexwaterfeatures.com

The following companies specialize in wind- and solar-powered aerators, water pumps, circulators, and deicers:

**Malibu Water Resources**
*See this page.*

**O'Brock Windmills**
*See this page.*

**Danner Manufacturing, Inc.**
160 Oval Drive
Islandia, NY 11749-1489
631-234-5261
www.pondmaster.com

## BRIDGES AND GAZEBOS

**BowBends**
P.O. Box 900
Bolton, MA 01740
978-779-6464
www.bowbends.com

**Dalton Pavilions, Inc.**
20 Commerce Drive
Telford, PA 18969
215-721-1492
www.daltonpavillions.com

**Vixen Hill Cedar Products**
Main Street
Elverson, PA 19520
800-423-2766
www.vixenhill.com
*Gazebos, architectural and garden ornaments.*

**Yardstuf, Inc.**
P.O. Box 32
La Marque, TX 77568
866-690-9273
www.gardenbridges.com
*Garden bridges.*

## EROSION-CONTROL BLANKETS AND MATS

These companies sell various soil protection reinforcements.

**Belton Industries, Inc.**
8613 Roswell Road
Atlanta, GA 30350
800-225-4099
www.beltonindustries.com

**BioFence**
15 Mohawk Avenue East
Freetown, MA 02717
508-763-5253
www.biofence.com

**Earth Saver**
R.H. Dyck, Inc.
P.O. Box 310
Yolo, CA 95697
866-WATTLES (928-8537)
www.earth-savers.com

**Indian Valley Industries, Inc.**
P.O. Box 810
Johnson City, NY 13790
800-659-5111
www.iviindustries.com

**Mat, Inc.**
12402 Highway 2
Floodwood, MN 55736
888-477-3028
www.soilguard.com

**North American Green**
14649 Highway 41 North
Evansville, IN 47725
800-772-2040
www.nagreen.com

**RoLanka International**
155 Andrew Drive
Stockbridge, GA 30281
800-760-3215
www.rolanka.com

**SI Corporation**
4019 Industry Drive
Chattanooga, TN 37416
800-621-1273
www.sind.com

**Ten Cate Nicolon**
365 South Holland Drive
Pendergrass, GA 30567
800-685-9990
www.tcnicolon.com

## FOUNTAINS

**Aquacenter, Inc.**
*See page 147.*

**Aqua Art**
7603 Toni Circle
Salt Lake City, UT 84121
801-815-1629
www.aquaartfountains.com
*Custom-made indoor and outdoor fountains.*

**Otterbine Barebo, Inc.**
*See page 148.*

**Stoney Creek Equipment Co.**
*See page 148.*

## GARDEN PONDS

**American Aquatic Gardens**
621 Elysian Fields Avenue
New Orleans, LA 70117
504-944-0410

**AquaMats**
Meridian Aquatic Technology
4041 Powder Mill road, Suite 205
Calverton, MD 20705
301-937-1240
www.aquamats.com
*Bio-habitat technology used to increase water clarity and improve fish and plant habitat.*

**Aquascape Designs, Inc.**
1200 Nagel Boulevard
Batavia, IL 60510
800-306-6227
www.aquascapedesigns.com
*Water-gardening catalog and services designed for professional landscape designers and pool installers. Prefers to deal wholesale.*

**Beckett Water Gardens**
5931 Campus Circle Drive
Irving, TX 75063
888-BECKETT (232-5388)
www.888beckett.com

**Laguna Koi Ponds**
20452 Laguna Canyon Road
Laguna Beach, CA 92651
949-494-5107
www.lagunakoi.com

**Maryland Aquatic Nurseries, Inc.**
3427 North Furnace Road
Jarrettsville, MD 20184
410-557-7615
www.marylandaquatic.com

**Moorehaven Water Gardens**
3006 York Road
Everett, WA 98204
425-743-6888
www.moorehaven.com

**Paradise Water Gardens**
14 May Street
Whitman, MA 02382
800-955-0161
www.paradisewatergardens.com

**Perry's Water Garden**
136 Gibson Aquatic Farm Road
Franklin, NC 28734
828-524-3264
www.perryswatergarden.net

**Scherer & Sons**
104 Waterside Road
Northport, NY 11768
613-261-7432

**Slocum Water Gardens**
1101 Cypress Gardens Boulevard
Winter Haven, FL 33884
863-293-7151

**Waterford Gardens**
74 East Allendale Road
Saddle River, NJ 07458
201-327-0721
www.waterfordgardens.com

**White Flower Farm**
P.O. Box 50
Litchfield, CT 06759
800-503-9264
www.whiteflowerfarm.com

**Van Ness Water Gardens**
2460 North Euclid Avenue
Upland, CA 91784
800-205-2425
www.vnwg.com

## Outdoor Furnishings and Ornaments

**Adirondack Wood Furnishings**
P.O. Box 608
Malone, NY 12953
800-280-1541
www.adirondackwoodfurnishings.com

**Frontgate**
8939 Union Centre Boulevard
Westchester, OH 45069
800-626-6488
www.frontgate.com
*Cataloger of upscale waterside furniture,
including a floating pool recliner for those
who find inner tubes too déclassé.*

**Gardener's Supply Company**
128 Intervale Road
Burlington, VT 05401
888-833-1412
www.gardeners.com

**Kenneth Lynch & Sons**
84 Danbury Road
P.O. Box 488
Wilton, CT 06897
203-762-8363
www.klynchandsons.com

**Plow and Hearth Catalog**
P.O. Box 5000
Madison, VA 22727-1500
800-627-1712
www.plowhearth.com

**Preferred Living Catalog**
Clermont County Airport
Batavia, OH 45103
800-776-7897
www.sportys.com
*Outdoor furniture and water toys.*

**Smith & Hawken**
#4 Hamilton Landing, Suite 100
Novato, CA 94949
800-940-1170
www.smith-hawken.com

## Pest Management

**Berkshire Biological**
264 Main Road
Westhampton, MA 01027
800-462-1382
www.berkshirebio.com
*Sells dragonfly larvae, which are used for
nontoxic mosquito control.*

**Bird-X**
300 North Elizabeth Street
Chicago, IL 60607
800-662-5021
www.bird-x.com
*Products to repel geese, heron, and other pests,
nonlethally. Latest product: a floating alli-
gator head replica "to guard your pond."*

**The Green Spot**
93 Priest Road
Nottingham, NH 03290
603-942-8925
www.greenmethods.com
*Sells mosquito dunks (a nontoxic bacterial
agent) and bat houses for mosquito control.*

## Piping and Outlet Systems

**Agri Drain Corporation**
1462 340th Street
P.O. Box 458
Adiar, IA 50002
800-232-4742
www.agridrain.com

**Pond Dam Piping, Ltd.**
398 Eighth Street
Macon, GA 31201
800-333-2611
www.ponddampiping.com

**Southeastern Pipe and Drain Systems**
P.O. Box 1282
Aiken, SC 29802
800-468-7564
www.sepipe.net

## SEED, ROOTSTOCK, AND PLANTS

**J&J Tranzplant Aquatic Nursery**
P.O. Box 227
Wild Rose, WI 54984-0227
800-622-5055
www.tranzplant.com
*Submergent and emergent plants, including some hard-to-find species like Jack-in-the-Pulpit and wild leek. Specializes in propagating, harvesting, and supplying submergent and emergent vegetation for wetland restoration, environmental, and land reclamation concerns.*

**Kester's Wild Game Food Nurseries, Inc.**
P.O. Box 516
Omro, WI 54963
920-685-2929
www.kestersnursery.com
*Excellent source of seed, rootstock, and plants. Order its catalog which is full of good information and makes a useful reference for wildlife attractants. One of the oldest wetland nurseries in the country.*

**Lilypons Water Gardens**
P.O. Box 10
Buckeystown, MD 21717
1-800-999-5459
www.lilypons.com
*Excellent selection of aquatics for natural ponds and water gardens. Catalog's color photos are excellent.*

**JFNew**
(formerly Prairie Ridge Nursery)
708 Roosevelt Road
Walkerton, IN 46574
574-586-3400
www.jfnew.com
*Propagated native plants and seeds for prairies, woodlands, and wetlands. Offers a wide variety of grasses and sedges for upland cover, as well as aquatics.*

**Wildlife Nurseries, Inc.**
P.O. Box 2724
Oshkosh, WI 54903-2724
920-231-3780
www.gardenwatchdog.com
*Wetland seeds and plants to attract waterfowl and other wildlife, as well as mallard nesting cylinders and wood-duck boxes. Exceptionally informative catalog with planting techniques and suggestions. A good source of plants for landscape architects and water gardeners, too. Nice selection of seeds, roots, and tubers for wetland improvement.*

**William Tricker, Inc.**
7125 Tanglewood Drive
Independence, OH 44131
1-800-524-3492
www.tricker.com
*Shallow-water and bog plants; also a large selection of plants for water gardens. America's oldest water garden specialist is a U.S. historic landmark, and worth a visit.*

## SOIL SEALANTS AND ARTIFICIAL MEMBRANES

**DLM Plastics**
1530 Harvard Avenue
Findlay, OH 45840
800-444-5877
www.dlmplastics.com

**Poly-Flex**
2000 West Marshall Drive
Grand Prairie, TX 75051
800-527-3322
www.poly-flex.com

**PondTechnology**
2633 North Calvert Street
Baltimore, MD 21218
800-477-7724
www.pondtechnology.com

**Reef Industries**
P.O. Box 750250
Houston, TX 77275-0250
800-231-2417
www.reefindustries.com

**Yunker Plastics**
251 O'Connor Drive
Elkhorn, WI 53121
800-236-3328
www.yunkerplastics.com

The following companies specialize in sealants for pervious soils:
CETCO
1500 West Shure Drive
Arlington Heights, IL 60004
800-527-9948
www.cetco.com
*Bentonite products.*

**CIM Industries**
23 Elm Street
Petcrborough, NH 03458
800-543-3458
www.cimindustries.com
*Liquid-applied rubber.*

**Seepage Control, Inc.**
P.O. Box 51177
Phoenix, AZ 85076-1177
800-214-9640
www.seepagecontrol.com
*Sells ESS-13, a resinous liquid-applied polymer emulsion.*

## SWIM RAFTS

**Follansbee Dock Systems**
P.O. Box 610
Follansbee, WV 26037
www.follansbeedocks.com

## WATER ANALYSIS EQUIPMENT

A number of companies offer water-testing equipment for harmful substances—bacteria, chemicals, synthetic organic compounds (such as pesticides), heavy metals, volatiles (such as gasoline), and more. However, each state sets its own parameters for acceptable limits, and many pond owners first contact their state health department for help with water testing. Private water analysis firms may be useful in offering a wide spectrum of tests, and quicker results, usually for a higher fee. Either way, local testing often makes sense because time can be a factor in assuring valid water samples. Check your yellow pages or the Internet for local water-testing services.

**Aquatic Eco-Systems, Inc.**
1767 Benbow Court
Apopka, FL 32703
800-422-3939
www.aquaticeco.com

**Hach Company**
P.O. Box 389
Loveland, CO 80539
800-227-4224
www.hach.com

**LaMotte**
P.O. Box 329
Chestertown, MD 21620
800-344-3100
www.lamotte.com

## WATER CONDITIONERS

**ABA**
Water Quality Science International, Inc.
P.O. Box 552
Bolivar, MO 65613
800-558-9442
www.wqsii.com

**Aquashade**
Cygnet Enterprises, Inc.
1860 Bagwell Street
Flint, MI 48503
800-359-7531
www.cygnetenterprises.com

**Aquatic Eco-Systems, Inc.**
*See page 148.*

**Lake Colorant WSP**
Becker-Underwood
801 Dayton Avenue
Ames, IA 50010
800-232-5907
www.beckerunderwood.com

**Natural Solutions**
P.O. Box 114
Keuka Park, NY 14478-0114
315-531-8803
www.naturalsolutionsetc.com
*Source of barley straw bundles for natural alga control.*

### WATERFOWL NESTING

**Cattail Products**
P.O. Box 309
Fulton, IL 61252
815-589-4230
www.cattailproducts.com
*Mallard cylinder nests.*

**Chesapeake Wildlife Heritage**
46 Pennsylvania Avenue
P.O. Box 1745
Easton, MD 21601
410-822-5100
www.cheswildlife.org

**Design Tanks**
1810 East Avenue
Sioux Falls, SD 57104
888-366-8265
www.design-tanks.com

**Wildlife Nurseries, Inc.**
*See page 152.*

# GOVERNMENT ORGANIZATIONS

**U.S. Army Corps of Engineers**
441 G Street, NW
Washington, DC 20314
202-761-0660
www.usace.army.mil
*The Army Corps of Engineers has regulatory power over some waterway work, which may include pond construction. To find out, contact your local U.S. Army Engineers district office.*

**U.S. Department of Agriculture Farm Service Agency**
P.O. Box 2415
Washington, DC 20013
202-690-0474
www.fsa.usda.gov
*The FSA administers many water programs and may provide financial support for agricultural water projects, depending on county priorities.*

**U.S. Department of Agriculture Natural Resources Conservation Service**
14th Street and Independence Avenue, SW
P.O. Box 2890
Washington, DC 20013
202-720-3210
www.nrcs.usda.gov
*Despite reductions in funding for pond design support, the NRCS (a new version of the former Soil Conservation Service) can be an excellent source of information regarding pond design, watershed calculation, and spillway requirements. Check your phone book for the NRCS office in your county.*

# MISCELLANEOUS

**The Land Improvement Contractors of America**
3060 Ogden Avenue, Suite 304
Lisle, IL 60532
630-548-1984
www.licanational.com
*Organization of conservation-minded earth-moving contractors. May be able to recommend a pond builder in your area.*

# INDEX

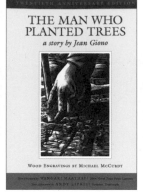

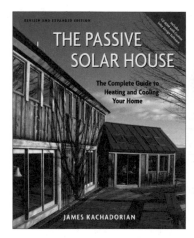
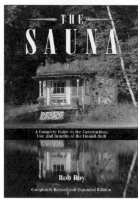
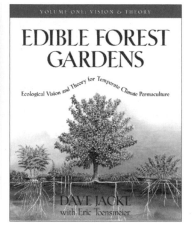